STANDING IN THE SHADOWS OF MOTOWN

THE LIFE AND MUSIC OF LEGENDARY BASSIST JAMES JAMERSON

BY DR. LICKS

A DOCTOR LICKS PUBLICATION

STANDING IN THE SHADOWS OF MOTOWN
The Life and Music of Legendary Bassist James Jamerson.
Copyright © 1989 by Dr. Licks.

All rights reserved. No part of this book may be reproduced or utilized in any form or by any means electronic or mechanical, including photocopying, recording, or by any information storage and retrieval system, without permission in writing from the publisher.

Inquiries should be addressed to:
Dr. Licks Publishing
327 Haverford Rd.
Wynnewood, Pa., 19096.

Library of Congress Catalog Card Number: 88-51904

Printed and distributed in the United States of America by Hal Leonard Publ. Corp. Milwaukee, WI.

DEDICATED TO

The Funk Brothers,
and to studio musicians everywhere.

CONTENTS

Acknowledgments	viii
Credits	x
Foreword	xii
Introduction	xiii

PART 1

Funky Beginnings	3
Don't Look Back	5
Five Bucks A Session (And A Bowl Of Soup)	12
Welcome To The Apollo	18
Igor & The Funk Brothers (Part One)	25
Igor & The Funk Brothers (Part Two)	29
We're In The Money	36
Stompin' At The Chit Chat	41
Don't Mess With James	46
Leave It To Jamerson	49
Dr. Jamerson & Mr. Hyde	52
Growing Pains	55
The Fall Of The King	65
Coda	76

PART 2

Anatomy Of A Sound	81
B-15's And Funk Machines	84
The Cast	87
Discography	88
Igor's Chromatic Exercise	91
An Appreciation Of The Style - by Anthony Jackson	92

PART 3

Stars And Scores	99
Tape Contents	101
Paul McCartney	102
James Jamerson Jr. (What's Going On, Ain't That Peculiar, My Guy)	103
Will Lee (I Heard It Through The Grapevine)	108
John Entwistle (Ain't Too Proud To Beg, Going To A Go-Go, Contract On Love)	111
Gerald Veasley (Darling Dear, You Can't Hurry Love, Shotgun)	113
Phil Chen (Reach Out, I'll Be There)	118
Pino Palladino (For Once In My Life, I Second That Emotion, I Know I'm Losing You)	121

Geddy Lee (Get Ready)	**125**
Chuck Rainey (Bernadette, Cloud Nine, You Keep Me Hanging On)	**127**
The Philadelphia Intl. Rhythm Section (Ain't No Mountain High Enough)	**132**
Freddy Washington (I'm Gonna Make You Love Me, Girl Why You Wanna Make Me Blue)	**136**
Garry Tallent (Baby Love)	**139**
Allen McGrier (It's A Shame)	**141**
John Patitucci (How Sweet It Is, Heat Wave, Mickey's Monkey)	**143**
Jimmy Haslip (Don't Mess With Bill, It's The Same Old Song, Shake Me Wake Me)	**147**
Bob Babbitt (Ain't Nothing Like The Real Thing, Uptight, I'm A Roadrunner)	**151**
Willie Weeks (Still Water, My Baby Loves Me)	**155**
David Hungate (Home Cookin')	**157**
Francis Rocco Prestia (Just A Little Misunderstanding)	**160**
Jack Bruce (Come 'Round Here, I'm The One You Need)	**162**
Kenny Aaronson (This Old Heart Of Mine, Strange I Know, Love Is Like An Itching In My Heart)	**164**
Marcus Miller (I Was Made To Love Her)	**168**
Nathan Watts (Nowhere To Run)	**171**
Non-Motown Medley	**174**
Basil Fearrington (Love Is Here And Now You're Gone, Since I Lost My Baby, I'm Wondering)	**175**
Anthony Jackson (How Long Has That Evening Train Been Gone)	**179**
Kudos	**183**
Bibliography	**191**

ACKNOWLEDGMENTS

Thanks to the following people for donating their time and knowledge to the interviews that are the foundation of this book:

Joe Messina, Johnnie Mae Matthews, Earl Van Dyke, Frank Wilson, Joe Hunter, Hank Cosby, Richard "Pistol" Allen, Eddie Willis, Gene Page, Uriel Jones, Jerry Steinholtz, Dennis Coffey, David T. Walker, Kenny Gradney, James Gadson, Thomas "Beans" Bowles, Eddie Holland, Brian Holland, Al McKay, Paul Riser, Melvin Franklin, Larry Tolbert, David Van dePitte, Eli Fontaine, Michael Henderson, Ben Barrett, Bob Babbitt, Ron Brown, Wah Wah Watson, Robert White, Evelina MacKnight, Johnny Bristol, Richard "Popcorn" Wylie, Grover Washington Jr., Mike McClain, Jack Bruce, Weldon McDougal, Maurice King, Jack Brokensha, Martha Jean "The Queen" Steinberg, Lawrence Horn, Kenny Koontz, Bobby Malach, Gil Askey, Smokey Robinson, Cllifford Mack, Martha Reeves, Freddie Perren, Don White, Andrew Smith, Andrew "Mike" Terry, Cornellus Grant, George McGregor, Horace "Chili" Ruth, Choker Campbell, Joe Weaver, David Hungate, the Jamerson family, Don Davis, Chuck Rainey, Hal Davis, Nelson George, and Ortheia Barnes.

Thanks to the following people for helping to recruit the guest artists on the tapes:

Victor Carstarphen, Reggie Hamilton, Barry Moorhouse of The Bass Center in London, Chris Moury of The Bass Center in Los Angeles, Dave Edmunds, Allen Crowder of MPL, Phil Chen, Howard Stern of KROC in New York City, James Jamerson Jr., Keith Benson, Allen Spivak and Larry Magid of Electric Factory Concerts, Bob Babbitt, Vinny and Joey of Fodera Basses, Anthony Jackson, Bibi Green of Project X, Chris Jisi, Evelyn of Mad Hatter studios, and GRP records.

Additional thanks to:

Richard Williams, Jerry Millendorf, Stan Slotter, Esther Edwards and Doris Holland of The Motown Historical Museum, Randy and Tim at Eight Street Music in Philly, "The Flounder," Bob Adler, Larry Stephans of Motown Record Corp., Berry Gordy, Rebecca Jiles, Vincent Perrone, and Rosalind Stevenson of The Gordy Co., Andy Rossi of Steinberger Basses, George Schureman, Hajwell (Word!), Don Snowden, Ken Smith, Maureen Stuart and Eddie Olewnik of PCI, Ilaria Arpino, Studio "A" in Dearborn Heights, Michigan, Tom Wheeler of *GUITAR PLAYER,* Matt Resnicoff of *GUITAR WORLD,* Sal Labruna, Dennis Nardi, Mark Knox, and Bob Rust of Strata, Richard Cocoo Jr. of Labella, John Grunder of Fender Musical Instruments, and the Majestics.

For services above and beyond the call of duty:

The Jamerson family for their constant encouragement and support, Anthony Jackson for your musical knowledge and friendship, Phil Chen for helping me to remember the innocence and excitement of being a fifteen year old kid with a musical hero, Basil Fearrington for the "psychiatric sessions," Gene Leone for your technical excellence and creative vision, my wife and parents for putting up with me, and all the bassists and other musicians who have contributed to this project.

Special thanks to the following people for helping with publicity:

Marshall Crenshaw, Scott Iseler of *MUSICIAN*, Chris Jisi, Dave Marsh of *ROCK & ROLL CONFIDENTIAL*, Tom Cossie of *THE R&B REPORT*, Blair Jackson of *MIX*, and Kelly Castleberry and Lisa Tabor of *INTERNATIONAL MUSICIAN*.

CREDITS

Researched and written by
Dr. Licks from June 1987 to December 1988.
Audio tape produced by Dr. Licks.

All score transcriptions by Dr. Licks except for the following:
1) "Reach Out, I'll Be There"—transcribed by Larry "G" Goldman
2) "What's Going On"—transcribed by Larry "G" Goldman and Dr. Licks
3) "I'm Wondering"—transcribed by Basil Fearrington
4) "How Long Has That Evening Train Been Gone"—transcribed by Anthony Jackson
5) "I'd Be A Fool Right Now"—transcribed by Anthony Jackson
6) "Uptight"—transcribed by Anthony Jackson

Text edited by: Joseph Valente, Jerry Millendorf,
Sal Labruna, Elaine Slutsky, and Rachel Slutsky
Music edited by: Jerry Millendorf, Sal Labruna,
Basil Fearrington, and Dr. Licks

Art design and concept by: Ilaria Arpino
Additional artwork: Amy Fisher, Patty Shea, Ray Frescino
Text and music typeset on the Macintosh SE by: Dr. Licks and Jack Faith

Music editing and tape assembly by: Gene C. Leone Jr. at Victory East studios
Assistant engineers: George Schureman and Robert (Haji) Kloss

All songs throughout *Standing in the Shadows of Motown* are
Copyright © Jobete Music Co. Inc. All rights reserved. Used by Permission.

The title, *Standing in the Shadows of Motown,* was inspired by a Nelson George
article that appeared in *MUSICIAN* magazine.

PHOTO CREDITS

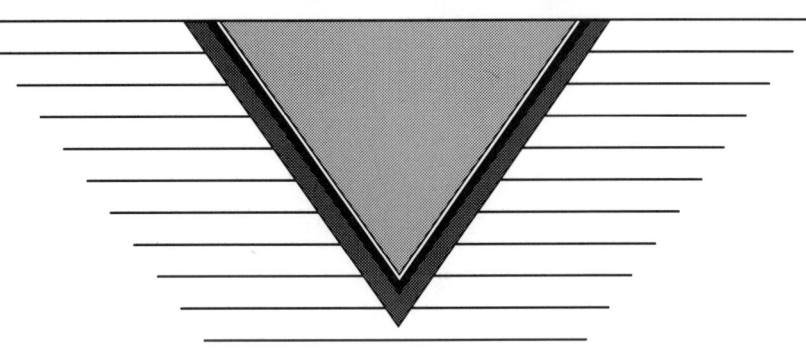

Page xii.	Courtesy of The Gordy Company
Page 6.	Courtesy of Annie Jamerson
Page 7.	Courtesy of Annie Jamerson
Page 8.	Courtesy of Annie Jamerson
Page 10.	Courtesy of Annie Jamerson
Page 11.	Courtesy of Little Sonny
Page 13.	Photo by Bob Adler
Page 14.	Courtesy of Annie Jamerson
Page 15.	Courtesy of Martha Reeves
Page 19.	Courtesy of the Motown Historical Museum (photo by Bob Adler)
Page 20	Courtesy of the Motown Historical Museum (photo by Bob Adler)
Page 21	Courtesy of the Motown Historical Museum (photo by Bob Adler)
Page 22.	Courtesy of Annie Jamerson
Page 23.	Courtesy of Annie Jamerson
Page 25.	Courtesy of Joe Messina, Annie Jamerson, and Eddie Willis
Page 26.	Courtesy of Earl Van Dyke
Page 28.	Courtesy of Earl Van Dyke
Page 30.	Courtesy of the Motown Historical Museum (photo by Bob Adler)
Page 33.	Courtesy of Earl Van Dyke
Page 34.	Courtesy of Earl Van Dyke
Page 37.	Courtesy of Earl Van Dyke
Page 39.	Courtesy of Earl Van Dyke
Page 40.	Courtesy of Annie Jamerson
Page 41.	Courtesy of Annie Jamerson
Page 42.	Photos courtesy of Annie Jamerson
Page 43.	Courtesy of Annie Jamerson
Page 44.	Photos courtesy of Earl Van Dyke
Page 47.	Courtesy of Annie Jamerson
Page 49.	Photo by Bob Adler
Page 50.	Courtesy of Annie Jamerson
Page 53.	Courtesy of Annie Jamerson
Page 57.	Left photo courtesy of Dennis Coffey
Page 57.	Right photo courtesy of Annie Jamerson
Page 59.	Courtesy of Annie Jamerson
Page 61.	Courtesy of Annie Jamerson
Page 62.	Courtesy of Annie Jamerson
Page 66.	Photos courtesy of Annie Jamerson
Page 67.	Photo by Bob Adler
Page 68.	Courtesy of Phil Chen
Page 69.	Courtesy of Phil Chen
Page 71.	Courtesy of Annie Jamerson
Page 72.	Courtesy of James Jamerson Jr.
Page 73.	Courtesy of Annie Jamerson
Page 75.	Courtesy of *GUITAR PLAYER* (photo by Jon Sievert)
Page 77.	Photos by Bob Adler
Page 81.	Courtesy of the Motown Historical Museum (photo by Bob Adler)
Page 82.	Courtesy of the Motown Historical Museum (photos by Bob Adler)
Page 84.	Photo by Bob Adler
Page 85.	Left photo courtesy of Phil Chen
Page 85.	Right photo by Bob Adler
Page 86.	Photo by Bob Adler
Page 88.	Photo by The Shooters
Page 92.	Photos by The Shooters
Page 96.	Courtesy of *GUITAR PLAYER* (photo by Jon Sievert)
Page 102.	Photo by Andy Beard (Globe Photos)
Page 103.	Photo by Christine "Peaches" Jamerson
Page 108.	Courtesy of Will Lee
Page 111.	Courtesy of John Entwistle
Page 113.	Courtesy of Ibanez
Page 118.	Photo by David Sessions
Page 121.	Courtesy of Pino Palladino
Page 125.	Courtesy of Steinberger Basses
Page 127.	Courtesy of Chuck Rainey
Page 132.	Photo by Scott Weiner
Page 136.	Courtesy of Ken Smith Basses.
Page 139.	Photo by Neal Preston
Page 141.	Courtesy of Allen McGrier
Page 143.	Courtesy of GRP records
Page 147.	Courtesy of Jimmy Haslip
Page 151.	Courtesy of Bob Babbitt
Page 155.	Courtesy of Willie Weeks
Page 157.	Courtesy of David Hungate
Page 160.	Courtesy of Rocco Prestia
Page 162.	Courtesy of Electric Factory Concerts
Page 164.	Photo by Ed Clarke
Page 168.	Courtesy of Patrick Rains & Associates
Page 171.	Courtesy of Nathan Watts
Page 175.	Photo by Scott Weiner
Page 179.	Photo by Ebet Roberts
Page 193.	Courtesy of Annie Jamerson
Page 194.	Courtesy of Earl Van Dyke

FOREWORD

James Jamerson was an incomparable bass player who pumped life blood into hundreds of our Motown hit records. Together with Benny Benjamin on drums, Robert White on guitar, and Earl Van Dyke on piano, they made up our inner circle of musicians for many years.

I am delighted that Jamerson's greatness is being realized outside of close music circles. The aptly named "Funk Brothers" were among the many geniuses we had under one roof. The world knows the superstars—Stevie Wonder, Michael Jackson, Diana Ross, Smokey Robinson, Marvin Gaye, and many others. However, the brilliance and innovativeness of James Jamerson was a major part of the magical combination that made their music the huge success that it was.

Jamerson, a man of few words, was proud and protective of his music. Only when I asked him to change something would he speak up, never mincing his words in defense of it. Even if he begrudgingly changed it to suit me, he'd find a way to turn it around to his liking. And . . . in many cases, I'd have to begrudgingly admit that his way was better.

There was a unique and special bond between drummer Benny Benjamin and Jamerson. It was awesome how they could get a lock-step interaction going. It would baffle today's computer experts. Hi-tech music couldn't compete with these guys when they got an honest and true groove going.

Jamerson always put his heart and soul into every song. When listening to our earlier Motown hits, it's easy to gain an appreciation for the man who revolutionized the artistry of the bass. There is hardly a successful pop band in the world that doesn't owe homage to James Jamerson. His influence is omnipotent.

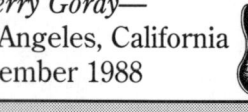

—*Berry Gordy*—
Los Angeles, California
September 1988

INTRODUCTION

Midway through NBC's 1983 airing of *Motown 25: Yesterday, Today, and Tomorrow*, Richard Pryor, in his own inimitable style, asked the musical question, "Exactly what is the Motown Sound? What, What, What?" Holland-Dozier-Holland, Berry Gordy, and other assorted Motown production people gave their versions of what they thought the recipe was, but the answer that hit home came from Smokey Robinson's satiny vocal chords: "Well, the Motown Sound is the bottom you know. They got the foot working and you can hear the bass real good." Well, just who was this mystery bassist who was so essential to one of the most influential musical formulas in the history of popular music?

He certainly wasn't the panic stricken bass player screaming out, "What key, what key?" during the reprise of Stevie Wonder's "Fingertips Part II;" and if you're looking for a synthesizer or a sequencer to be the answer to this puzzle, forget it because there never has been and never will be a machine that could possibly have that much soul. So after all this Hollywood buildup, you're expecting a big star to step forward right? Well, if I spill the beans at this point and say, "It was James Jamerson," 98 percent of the general reading public is probably going to say, "James who?" Don't feel bad—even a lot of bass players have no idea who he is.

So why have 25 world famous musicians donated their time and talents to honor some unknown musician who was just another studio bass player? Well for starters, saying that James Jamerson was just another studio bass player is like saying that Baryshnikov is just another dancer, or Picasso was just another painter. For a decade and a half, James' driving bass lines did a lot more than just provide the rocket fuel that propelled the Motown hit machine. Throughout the '60s, when "The Way You Do the Things You Do" was causing teenage males in every urban center in the country to try and learn the "Temptations Walk," and Smokey was busy crooning to millions of back seat sweethearts about the virtues of eternal love, James' musical offerings were reaching out to a completely different audience. Across the globe, his innovations on his Fender Precision caused bassists to run for their turntables, as they scratched their way through Motown records and annihilated their phonograph needles in vain attempts to figure out just what this unknown musician was doing. Bassist John Entwistle summed up the situation perfectly when he said, "I didn't know that it was James Jamerson. I just called him the guy who played bass for Motown, but along with every other bassist in England, I was trying to learn what he was doing."

Researching this book has not been the usual "get the facts and write a story" type of procedure. At times, it seemed to me as if I was caught in the midst of a detective or spy novel as I tried to sort things out. Some of these events happened almost thirty years ago and "The Jamerson Legend" amongst some of his peers has grown in proportion to the time passed. Initially, the constant conflicts and contradictions that kept surfacing throughout the interviews were extremely frustrating and confusing. As I unsuccessfully tried to explain and rationalize all the inconsistencies by attributing them to time, faulty memory, or different perspectives, I began to realize what all the people I interviewed had been trying to tell me. The conflicts and contradictions were a mirror image of Jamerson's life and music.

Throughout this book, you will notice an overabundance of direct quotes from James' friends, family, and assorted center stage and "behind the scenes" Motown figures. In the period during which I was conducting the interviews and digging into Jamerson's past, I was amazed by how easily the facts poured out—contradictions and all. On a rainy night in November of '87 while James' widow and I were visiting a local Detroit club called Dummy George's, I found out why. The featured act that night was the Jimmy Wilkins Orchestra, a smokin' big band in the vein of Basie, Ellington, and Woody Herman. Most of the players were old veterans of Motown's glory days in Studio A, and they were more than willing—almost eager—to talk about James and their individual roles in Motown's rich history. No matter how their lives may have turned out after Motown's departure from Detroit, there was the gleam of youth in their eyes this particular night as they recounted their stories of three o'clock in the morning sessions in the steamy, smoke filled environment of "Hitsville U.S.A." It was an era of magic, and hope, and dreams, that none of them would ever trade for any amount of money.

Rather than try to interpret what they've said, I've chosen to quote James' friends and transmit their thoughts and memories exactly as they were originally told to me. There is a certain quality of earthy eloquence in their words that this writer could never match; besides, it was too much fun initially listening to them to risk watering down their tales and comments with an outsider's point of view. I hope and feel that the same honesty and freshness of these conversations will be conveyed to the reader

This is not the first attempt to chronicle Jamerson's life and music. Motown musicians and music directors like Cornelius Grant and Maurice King made futile attempts at convincing James to write down what he was doing so that it wouldn't be lost, but at the time, he was too busy creating to worry about posterity. When he finally realized the importance of what his friends had been telling him, it was too late. Prior to his tragic death in 1983, James was trying in vain to interest the media in his story. But with the exception of *BILLBOARD's* Nelson George and *GUITAR PLAYER's* Dan Forte, there were very few takers.

Obviously, a good portion of this book is dedicated to an in depth study of one of the most difficult and influential of all pop bass styles. At first glance, thumbing through the pages and seeing all the musical scores, it would appear that this is a technical book that is exclusively directed at electric bassists. Nothing could be further from the truth. It is also a story of a time when there was a human being with a unique personality playing each instrument—a period of musical innocence when comraderie and fun were more important than money and hype. For Motown enthusiasts, this book will give you a behind the scenes look at who the musicians were and what actually happened during those historic recording sessions. And above all, the story of one of Motown's most creative and enigmatic personalities will finally be told.

Funky Beginnings

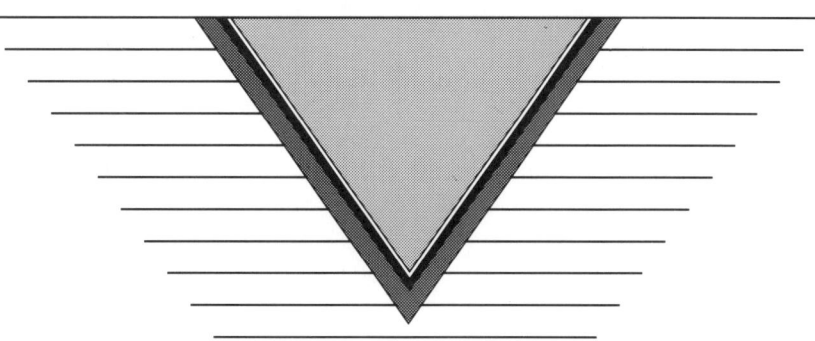
FUNKY BEGINNINGS

> *"I used to go out behind the house where there were all these ants on the ground, and I would take a stick and stretch a long rubber band across it and play for the ants. I would make the ants dance."*

In the last year of his life, James Jamerson would relate this tale of his earliest encounter with the bass to one of his friends in Los Angeles. It seems a fitting overture to the story of a musician whose entire being and destiny were so completely wrapped up in the instrument that he played. Ordinarily, biographies begin with birthdates and birthplaces, but "the Jamerson Saga" is anything but ordinary. From day one, his life would begin to travel the strange and unpredictable path that would eventually lead him to musical glory and an inevitable tragic finish.

James' original birthdate was January 29, 1938, but in the late seventies, after seeing his birth certificate for the first time, he discovered, much to his dismay, that he had lost two years out of his life. He was actually born on January 29, 1936. Like many of our greatest Rhythm and Blues stars, James was born in the Deep South. The setting for his childhood and the mystical backyard where he eventually became the "Pied Piper of the ant world," was Charleston, South Carolina. His father, James Jamerson Sr., worked in the local shipyards, and his mother, Elizabeth, was a domestic.

Following his parents' early divorce, James' musical psyche would begin to emerge during a period when he was being shuffled back and forth between the households of his grandmother and his aunt. His grandmother played some piano and his aunt sang in the local church choir, but James' most important childhood influence was the piano at his cousin Louise's house. James would go there every day to practice, and by the age of ten, he had taught himself to play well enough to perform at the church and at local fish fries. He also studied trombone for a short time at his elementary school, but his discovery of the instrument that would create musical history was still five years down the road. Although James would not lay his hands on a "real bass" until he was almost sixteen, music had become a major passion in his life at a very early age. His aunt, Evalina MacKnight, recalls a daily ritual of telling him to turn off the radio in his bedroom and go to sleep. He was fascinated with all the local Gospel, Blues, and Jazz stations that flooded the airwaves around Charleston.

James' aunt knew from the beginning that he was very different. His school teachers also realized his potential and told her on several occasions that "He was going to be something special someday." Although he was a better than average student and a respectful and well-behaved child, he led a very isolated existence. The occasional games and sports that James played with his older brother Richard and some of his local friends were sporadic at best. Usually, he would be off somewhere by himself. The dual nature of his personality which would become more apparent through the years, also began to develop at an early age. On the surface, he seemed to be somewhat of a lighthearted prankster with a devilish smile and a great sense of humor, but there was always a very serious side to James Jamerson.

The realities of life were thrust upon him shortly before his tenth birthday, when a bicycle accident left him with both feet so badly crushed and mangled that the local doctors considered amputation. Fortunately, a bone specialist was able to successfully perform reconstructive surgery, but James was left with a slight limp and a sense of self-consciousness about his feet that would remain with him throughout his life. Following a year in a wheelchair, it would always be necessary for James to wear high-topped shoes or boots so that his feet and ankles would have sufficient support. In later years, his "bad wheels" would make him the brunt of jokes played upon him by the Motown studio musicians, but James usually had the good sense and humor to take it in stride.

The wounds left by the trauma of handling his skin color at an early age were not so easily healed. The Deep South of the early 1940's was not the best of all possible worlds for a young fair skinned black child with blue eyes. James' light complexion caused him to feel that he was an outcast to his darker friends and family. The insecurities and sense of isolation that developed from his broken home, and the feeling that he was too light to be black and too dark to be white, would have a great deal to do with the development of the side of his personality that made people refer to him as a loner. Looking for something that knew no color boundaries—something that he could throw himself into which would be all his—Jamerson headed for Detroit . . .
and a date
with a
bass.

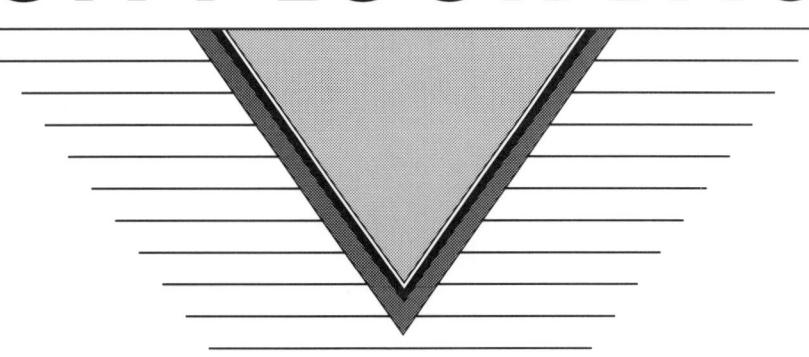

DON'T LOOK BACK

The sad events of Jamerson's childhood would always stay with him, but once he moved up north to Detroit, they were temporarily put on the back burner. There were just too many new friends to meet, and much too much music happening for him to remain preoccupied with exorcising the demons of his youth. By 1953, the pieces of James' musical puzzle were beginning to come together. Motown's founder, Berry Gordy, would officially enter the music business that summer by opening up his 3-D Record Mart. It would also be the year that James' mother would break ground for his northern migration, by moving to Detroit in search of employment. James was sent for during the following summer of 1954, a year that would prove to be an important turning point for him, because it was during this period that he would meet the two loves of his life—his future wife, and the bass.

In 1951, Annie Wells and her family had moved from Mississippi to a middle class neighborhood on Detroit's west side. It wasn't long before most of the neighborhood boys were flirting and competing for her attention, but no one was able to catch her eye until she had been living in Detroit for several years. While she was playing hopscotch one day, the new kid on the block, who was called "Snuffy" by his friends, was checking her out through the picket fence that surrounded his house. Her first thoughts upon seeing James' wide grin with his chipped tooth was, "Why is that snaggletooth staring at me?" Still, she found herself being strongly attracted to his rugged good looks and mischievous smile. Once James finally worked up the courage to introduce himself, they became inseparable. James always had bad diction and was overly self-conscious when it came to expressing himself. Annie learned about this on their second date when James boldly informed her, "Someday, I'm going to marriage you." While he may have been unsure of his enunciation, he definitely knew what he had in mind concerning Annie, because they were married shortly before his graduation from high school.

James was not quite as decisive about the selection of his musical instrument. When he enrolled at Detroit's Northwestern High, he knew that he wanted to learn another instrument besides piano, but he had no preconceived idea that it would be a bass. His high school buddy, drummer Clifford Mack explains, "We were walking down the hallway going in the same direction, and after a while we both realized we were headed for the same place. James introduced himself and said to me, 'Are you going to the music room too?,' and I said, 'Yeah.' Well, when we got there, we started checking out different instruments trying to figure what we wanted to play, and after a while, James noticed the upright bass laying on the floor in the back of the room. He picked it up and started strummin' it and he said, 'I'll be playing this within six months.'"

In later years, James would claim that Dr. Helstein, who was the music teacher at Northwestern, told him to choose upright bass as his instrument because he had large hands. According to Clifford, "Dr. Helstein was a good teacher but we didn't care for his personality very much. If he had something to tell you, he would come down on you hard and disgrace you. He was a good teacher but he wasn't very well-liked."

One of the most puzzling tasks connected with the researching of Jamerson's high school years, was trying to find someone who could recall an incubation period during which James was learning the bass. Musicians always have to struggle, at least for a brief period of time, when they learn a new instrument. At a minimum, it's necessary to develop enough basic motor skills so that the sound that your fingers or mouth produce can be called music, as opposed to being just uncontrolled vibrations

Don't Look Back

> James Jameson
> Comp 3
> Aug. 13, 1956
>
> **My Ambition**
>
> My desire is to become a great musician. I have always liked music ever since I could understand music, but I never have liked "rock + roll" because it didn't make sense to me. I consider that kind of music just a lot of noise. I have always wanted to play the piano by music instead of playing by ear, but instead of learning how to play the piano, I have learned to play the string bass. After finishing high school, I am planning to go to college and to major in music, and after the years that are required for a musician, I will teach music privately at home and at a school. I like music, because music is an easy subject, and it comes easier to me than any other subjects and that is why most of my time is spent when I am at home I practice on both instruments, the piano and the string bass to improve more in music.

Did you ever wonder what goes on in the mind of a young musical genius? James wrote this composition for his high school English class in 1956. It's ironic that the man who influenced so many Rock and Pop musicians spent his teenage years regarding Rock and Roll as "a lot of noise . . . that didn't make sense."

> **My Ambition**
>
> My desire is to become a great musician. During my time in elementary school, I didn't know anything about music but I have always wanted to know how to play an instrument. The only instrument I was interested in, was the piano, but instead of learning to play the piano, I learned how to play the string bass. I have always like all type of music except rock & roll in otherwords I called it "rockhouse." I am planing after finishing high school, too go to college. After the require years to be a musican, I will teach music because I think music is the better subject to teach in any schools, because the teacher wouldn't have no home work to correct. Music is a subject that come easier to me and most of my interest in music.

Maybe James would have received a better grade on his composition if his teacher had seen the gem that appeared in the rough draft above. The next to last sentence reads, "I will teach music because I think music is the better subject to teach in any schools, because the teacher wouldn't have no homework to correct."

of strings or air columns. However, it seemed that everyone I interviewed maintained that James just picked up the bass and started to make music from the moment his fingers touched the neck.

This is not meant to imply that he didn't practice. On the contrary, he was very dedicated and studious, but Jamerson's method of practicing was based upon constantly playing and performing with other musicians. He was not the type of musician who locked himself in a room and played scales all day long. Motown lyricist Eddie Holland, and James' lifelong friend, pianist Joe Weaver, both recounted stories of always seeing Jamerson running off somewhere to go to a rehearsal or a jam session when all the rest of his friends were hanging out or playing sports. Pianist Richard "Popcorn" Wylie's first encounter with Jamerson in 1955 illustrates just how far his musical skills and attitudes had progressed after only one year of playing the bass:

"One day, I was passing by this classroom and I heard these two guys playing. One of the janitors in the high school played piano just like Erroll Garner, and Jamerson was playing the bass with him exactly like it should be played along with the Erroll Garner style. You see, when James would practice, he would play jazz figures from guys like Ray Brown and Paul Chambers."

Not everything about James' high school years was serious. Shortly after arriving from South Carolina, he quickly made new friends and assumed the role of "class clown," a position that he would also hold down at the Motown studio. "He covered up for his inability to speak well by being comical and acting crazy and speakin' all stupid," acknowledges Clifford Mack. "He would do or say anything when he felt like it. He loved a good laugh. I used to tell him, 'Man, you bold! How the hell do you do that shit and get away with it?' I don't know if he became a comic to cover up his inability to speak fluently, but he could never have been a Martin Luther King or a Jesse Jackson."

Some of James' other lifelong non-musical (but non-crazy) passions would also have their origins during his stay at Northwestern. He began lifting weights and dabbling in karate, and he even played halfback for the football team one year, bad feet and all. And of course, cruising around the neighborhood with the boys was always good

James' high school jazz band with Roy Brooks on drums and an unidentified piano player.

for a few laughs, but it was Detroit's musical renaissance of the mid-50's that would occupy most of young Jamerson's time.

On any given night in local clubs like the West End, Klines, the Minor Key, and the Stimson Hotel, the experience of playing with some of Detroit's finest jazz musicians was available to anyone who could cut the mustard. Veterans like Barry Harris, Kenny Burrell, Hank Jones, and Yusef Lateef would take young aspiring jazz players like Jamerson or future Motown keyboardist Earl Van Dyke, and teach them the ropes. Sometimes, marathon bebop jam sessions would extend over an entire weekend at the houses of some of these musicians. Earl reminisces:

"Musicians at that time in Detroit used to get together socially on weekends and they would teach each other tunes and exchange ideas. We didn't compete with each other. For instance, Barry Harris taught me how to play 'Cherokee,' and he had learned it from another Detroit jazz musician named Hank Jones."

By 1957, James was steadily earning a reputation amongst the younger generation of Detroit musicians as an upcoming hot-shot bassist. Playing in bands with his friends, Popcorn and Clifford, James' schedule was kept very busy by playing local dances, weddings, clubs, and college fraternity parties. The camaraderie and friendly rivalries in these high school bands drove all three of the musicians to greater heights. Popcorn became the songwriter and performer who penned the smash hits, "With this Ring" and "Washed Ashore" for the Platters. Clifford would have a long and successful performing career as a drummer with Ramsey Lewis, Lou Rawls, and Groove Holmes. "We would ride each other when we were playing," laughs Clifford. "I would yell at James and challenge him, 'Man, keep the bass line going! Don't screw it up!' Then he would get on me."

By the twelfth grade, the demand for Jamerson's musical services had grown to the point where he was becoming somewhat of a legend in his neighborhood, because people constantly saw him driving from gig to gig with his big upright bass hanging halfway out of the car window. After the Detroit police department issued the underage Jamerson a permit so that he could freelance in clubs serving alcohol, he became even busier.

James was very bright but he was never the greatest of students. He didn't pay that much attention to his education because he didn't have to. He always knew that his bass playing would pull him through. When Wayne State University offered him a music scholarship upon his graduation from Northwestern, James realized that he was already busier than most of the teachers in their music department. Combined with the fact that Annie was pregnant with their first child, James declined the scholarship and opted for supporting his family with his already considerable musical skills. Besides, his high school goal of becoming a music teacher had long since shifted to dreams of being a world famous jazz musician, and he felt that he wasn't going to learn that in any school.

Shortly after his graduation, Jamerson would buy the first and only upright bass that he would ever own (for about $200). He also began his first steady club gig with a blues band called Washboard Willie and the Supersuds of Rhythm. "Willie played an actual washboard with cymbals on his fingers, a bass drum and a sock cymbal on the side," describes Clifford Mack. "There was also a guitar player in the band. It was a gimmick but it got over and you couldn't get in the club when they were playing. There were lines around the corner." Up until the beginning of 1958, James would play with Willie all over Detroit and Pontiac, in clubs like the Caribbean Lounge, the Apex, the Calumet Lounge, and the elegantly named "Bucket of Blood Club."

At the time, his tenure in this band didn't seem to be any more important than any other musical engagement, but it would actually have two profound effects on his life—one good, and one bad. The positive aspect of working with Willie was that James' bass playing abilities improved a great deal. Beans Bowles, studio saxophonist and manager of the early Motown Revues explains, "Washboard Willie played in all the natural blues keys like E, G, A, and D, and then when Jamerson went and played with anybody else, he played in all the other flat and sharp keys. Because of this, he became fluent on his entire instrument at a very early age." The bad side of life as a Supersud, was that James picked up some bad habits. The alcohol problem which would plague him throughout the rest of his life had its origins in this band. Up until this point, Jamerson had never touched a drop of liquor. In fact, his wife and friends insist that the teenage Jamerson was adamantly opposed to drinking, drugs,

Twenty-two year old James Jamerson with his brand new upright bass, playing with Washboard Willie and the Supersuds of Rhythm. The guitarist with the great looking Stratocaster is Mack Chimse. This shot was taken on Sept. 25, 1958.

and smoking.

The Detroit recording scene in the late 50's revolved around a collection of small independent labels that were struggling to stay afloat in the same waters as United Artists, RCA, Capitol, Mercury and the rest of the recording industry giants that operated out of New York, Los Angeles, and Chicago. The locals were always on the prowl for new recording talent in hopes of competing with "the big boys." One night in 1958, Johnnie Mae Matthews, who owned the local Northern Records label, happened to hear Jamerson playing in a club with Washboard Willie. His bass playing must have made a strong impression on her, because she hired him on the spot to record with some of the artists that she was producing at the time.

Playing behind Timmy Shaw, Betty Lavette, and the rest of the singers in Johnnie Mae's stable, James quickly began to make a name for himself in the local recording scene (not to mention the 10 to 20 dollars that he earned for each side that he cut) "After the first few sessions that he recorded for me," remarked Johnnie Mae, "James started to get in demand all over the city because unlike most of the bassists around town, he had his own style." Shortly after she hired James for his first recording date, Fortune, Tri-Phi, Anna Records (run by Berry Gordy's sister, Gwen), and all the rest of Detroit's small independent record companies and recording studios began to seek his expertise when they needed a bassist to record with their acts.

By mid-1958, James' recording career was by no means in full swing, but he was one of the biggest fish in the small pond that was Detroit's studio scene. Nevertheless, the ten to twenty dollars that he was earning from his live engagements and recording sessions was not the kind of money that bought houses. To generate more income, Jamerson began filling in the holes in his schedule with extra club dates with local acts like blues harmonica player, Little Sonny, and singer, J.J. Barnes. Still, James, Annie, and their newborn son, James Jr., would have to live with his mother until 1961, when his wages increased enough to enable him to move his family into a small apartment on the West Side. The Washboard Willie experience had taken him just about as far as it could, but it had been more than enough. When a few local musicians who had seen his Supersuds routine asked him to observe a recording session at a small studio at 2648 West Grand Boulevard, he had no idea that this career move would eventually push his bass playing into the international spotlight.

Playin' the blues with Little Sonny. This shot was taken in 1962 at the Apex bar in Detroit. From left to right are Jamerson, Little Sonnny, guitarist Robert Kimball, and drummer James Crawford.

FIVE BUCKS A SESSION

(AND A BOWL OF SOUP)

Precisely when and how James came to Motown is a mystery that is lost and buried somewhere down in old Studio "A" amongst the ghosts of recording sessions past. Early guitarist Don Davis, producer-saxophonist Hank Cosby, and keyboardists Joe Hunter and Popcorn Wylie have all been credited by different people as being the person who introduced James to the basement studio at 2648 West Grand Boulevard. Despite all the uncertainty, there is one fact that everyone agrees upon. Although James is the unquestioned "King of Motown Bass," he was definitely not the first to lay down a groove for Berry Gordy. Clarence Isabell, Tweed Beard, Willie Green, and a high school principal named Professor Joe Williams all preceded him. In fact, Professor Williams played on Marv Johnson's "Come to Me," which is the record that is considered to be the birth of Motown. However, Berry's thirst for perfection was apparently not satisfied by any of these players, because they quickly became history when Jamerson arrived on the scene.

The title of James' first Motown track is also an image that has long since faded from the minds of Motown's original studio crowd, but the impression that he made on everyone who watched his initial company recording date will never be forgotten. Early Motown bandleader Joe Hunter narrates:

"Jamerson came into the studio with Hank Cosby and he was just standing on the side watching Tweed Beard struggling with the song we were cutting at that sesssion. Somebody pointed to James and said, 'This is a good bass player here,' and they said, 'Man, come on and try this thing out.' James picked up Mr. Beard's upright bass and played the damn thing so good, everybody said, 'Shit, that's it!' Mr. Beard almost had a heart attack 'cause he knew he just lost the gig."

Although the musicians instantly took to James' style of bass playing, Motown's production team was not quite sure what to make of him. Popcorn Wylie explains:

"At first, they said that James played too busy because Motown didn't understand the sound that he was trying to bring in. They wanted a straight one and two and one and two . . . almost a Lawrence Welk feel with a lot of tambourine and loud guitar. The band that I brought in with Jamerson (Popcorn and the Mohawks) had a much more aggressive sound. We didn't convince them until after the different promotion and A&R guys from other companies like Chess and United Artists stopped by the studio and said, 'Hey, this guy has really got something.'"

The "something" that James had was the ability to incorporate his jazz backround into Berry Gordy's R&B influenced pop format. Although his early Motown bass work was nowhere near the mature late sixties style that would ultimately evolve in masterpieces like "Bernadette" and "I Was Made to Love Her," James was quickly setting himself apart from most of the bassists in the R&B industry. Gone were the stagnant two beat, root-fifth patterns and post-"Under the Boardwalk" clichéd bass lines that occupied the bottom end of most R&B releases. Jamerson had modified or replaced them with chromatic passing tones, Ray Brown style walking bass lines, and syncopated eighth-note figures—all of which had previously been unheard of in popular music of the late fifties and early sixties.

While James' widow Annie claims that he played on some of Gwen Gordy's 1958 Anna Records sessions and some of the early dates produced by Berry Gordy and his second wife, Raynoma, the first important hit that can definitely be credited to Jamerson and his new sound was the 1959 Miracles recording of "Way Over There." Even though this record would eventually only sell 60,000 copies, it was significant because it was Smokey Robinson's first solo production. It was also the Miracles' first release on Berry Gordy's independent Tamla label. While it's impossible to ignore the influence of all the bassists that James had previously heard on 50's hits by the Drifters, the Coasters, and the rest of the R&B world, the subtle distinctions between their lines and the syncopated chromatic style that he brought to his repetitive two bar vamp on "Way Over There" illustrate how he was already beginning to stretch the boundaries of R&B bass playing.

Like most of the tracks that James played on throughout 1959 and 1960, "Way Over There" was recorded with his upright bass. By 1961, James had switched over to the Fender bass for most of his work, but the upright would always remain his first love. Some of the studio musicians recall James sometimes playing his acoustic on a track and then overdubbing his electric on top of it for added punch. He could double his first line so closely that it was often difficult to tell that there were two basses on the same cut. Even though his reputation was built on his electric bass playing, throughout his Motown career, Jamerson would occasionally try to convince some of Motown's producers to let him return to his acoustic bass for a few selected tunes. The end results were usually worth his efforts because some of these upright inspired songs turned out to be Martha and the Vandellas' "Heat Wave," Stevie Wonder's "A Place in the Sun," and the Supremes' "Baby Love."

When James first came on the Motown scene in 1959, Berry Gordy's future empire was gathering steam but by no means was it in full swing. In 1957 and '58, Gordy's songwriting talents had earned him a modest degree of success after co-writing "Reet Petite," "That's Why," "I'll Be Satisfied," and "Lonely Teardrops" for Brunswick Records' Jackie Wilson. Always the perfectionist, Berry's quest for more control over the finished recordings of his compositions would eventually force him to become his own producer. Working out of his house and recording in different local studios like United Sound, Berry would write and produce tracks for future Motown stars like Eddie Holland, Marv Johnson, and the Miracles, and then lease them to small labels for distribution. Although the musical and business experience that Berry had accumulated through these productions was priceless, his net worth after all his efforts was not much more than when he had started. Chasing down record companies for royalties was not exactly what he had in mind for himself. Rising to the challenge of this dismal situation, Berry borrowed $700 from his family, bought a used two-track recording machine, opened up his own publishing company and record label, and shortly thereafter purchased the house at 2648 West Grand Boulevard that would eventually become known as "Hitsville U.S.A."

Keeping his head above water on the strength of sales from 1959 and 1960 hits like Barrett Strong's "Money," Marv Johnson's "Come to Me," and some of the early Miracles recordings like "You Can Depend on Me," Berry was gradually able to raise the pay scale of his studio musicians from the initial $5 a side to $7.25, $10, $15, and eventually several years later, the union scale of $52.50 a session. (Keyboardist Earl Van Dyke claims to have once been paid for an early Motown session with a

2648 West Grand Boulevard, Hitsville, U.S.A. Until the mid-sixties, all of Motown's recording and front office operations were centered exclusively in this building. The right hand door is the entrance to Studio "A."

bowl of soup.) Unfortunately, along with Berry's new stars, there were too many marginal acts signed to his label like Henry Lumpkin, the Satintones, Mabel John, and Singin' Sammy Ward, whose record sales were minimal. Even though the studio musicians could sense that something important was evolving in Berry's small basement studio, they still had to eat. There just was not enough recording going on to remain, so when Jackie Wilson had an opening for a new road band, James and a handful of other musicians in Berry's stable took a leave of absence and headed for greener pastures.

While it may seem as if James and his friends jumped ship at a crucial time when Berry Gordy needed them, this was actually not the case. The seemingly endless conveyor belt of hits that would pour out of Motown within a few short years was just a dream in early 1961. None of the studio musicians were signed to contracts at the time, and Motown was really nothing more than a part time job that would surface every so often when Berry Gordy or one of his other producers had a new song that required their services. Anyway, Berry didn't exactly sit on his hands waiting for James and his friends to come off the road. There were other musicians in Detroit.

As it turned out, the Jackie Wilson period was not much of an improvement over James' previous situation. Wilson was recovering from a gunshot wound inflicted by one of his crazed female admirers, so the amount of performing that he was able to do was limited. In his weakened condition, his frenzied, high-energy act just took too much out of him to risk performing more than three times a week. The musicians, who were being paid $25 a show, were living at the old Alvin Hotel at 52nd and Broadway, because Jackie's center of operations was New York. Well, it may not have been the greatest job in the world, but being able to send home $75 a week while working with one of the hottest Rhythm and Blues acts in the world doesn't sound too bad for 1961, right? . . . Wrong! The musicians also had to pay their own hotel bill which was $60 a week. On top of only clearing the grand sum of $15 a week, Jackie's business manager began to get "funny with the money," so James and the rest of the musicians were back in Detroit within a few months.

Jamerson's Jackie Wilson stint would not be the last time that he would moonlight while working for Motown.

Jamerson laying down a groove with Jackie Wilson. This shot was taken at a concert in Milford, Delaware in 1961. Mike Terry is the baritone sax player at the far right, Larry Veeder is the guitarist on the left, and Jamerson is in the center. The rest of the musicians are unidentified.

In later years, even while under contract, James would occasionally risk being fined in order to record for different studios and record labels both in Detroit and other neighboring cities. Prior to 1962, James' most frequent outside dates were with Thelma records (owned by Berry Gordy's first wife) and Harvey Fuqua's Tri-Phi and Harvey labels, but he also made a few trips to Chicago where he recorded for VeeJay and Brunswick. Probably the most famous of these early Chicago sessions was his 1961 meeting with blues legend, John Lee Hooker. Saxophonist Hank Cosby recollects:

"We had just come off the road with Jackie Wilson. I think we had an eight piece band, and this guy contacted us to do a date in Chicago. That was our first big date. It went to #12 on the pop charts." The record that came out of this session was 'Boom, Boom, Boom.'"

By late 1960, many of the components of Berry's dream studio band of the future were in place. Joe Hunter, Motown's first important bandleader and pianist, had been with Berry since the beginning. Joe would leave by late 1963, but not before lending his keyboard and arranging expertise to early hits like Marvin Gaye's "Pride and Joy," Martha and the Vandellas' "Heat Wave," and the Miracles' "Shop Around." Drummer Benny Benjamin had been recording for Berry since the "Come To Me" session and would eventually become a Motown trademark with his electrifying fills and pickups. Hitsville's main trio of guitar players had all arrived on the scene by 1960. Marv Johnson snatched Eddie Willis right out of high school in 1959. Robert White would arrive later that year after being stranded in Detroit at the end of a tour with Harvey Fuqua and the New Moonglows (which featured a young singer-drummer named Marvin Gaye). And direct from *The Soupy Sales Show,* Joe Messina showed his face (without pie on it) in 1960 and would probably play over 2,000,000 backbeats during the next thirteen years. Future Motown studio pianist, Earl Van Dyke, would run into James and the rest of the Detroit musicians in Jackie Wilson's backup band while he was touring with Lloyd Price in 1961. Complaining about the hardships of life on the road, all the musicians made plans for moving back home, but Earl would go out to play an additional Aretha Franklin tour before coming to Motown at the end of the year.

Although the rhythm section players usually got most of the glory down in the studio, much of the musical excitement that was generated on some of Motown's early releases must be attributed to the soul-stirring saxophone solos of Hank Cosby and Mike Terry. Hank, who would later go on to become one of Stevie Wonder's most important producers and co-writers through the mid-sixties, can be heard wailing away with his tenor sax on Gladys Knight and the Pips' "I Heard It Through the Grapevine," the Miracles' "Going to a GoGo," and the Temptations' "Get Ready." Mike Terry's contributions to the early and middle period Hitsville sessions are often overlooked, but his backround and solo work

The Joe Hunter band. Clockwise from the lower left: Benny Benjamin on drums, Jamerson, Joe Hunter, Hank Cosby on tenor sax, Mike Terry on baritone, and guitarist Larry Veeder in the center. These were the members of Motown's early studio lineup who took a leave of absence to play with Jackie Wilson.

on songs like the Four Tops' "Can't Help Myself," the Supremes' "I Hear a Symphony," and the Isley Brothers' "This Old Heart of Mine" would become as much a part of Motown as sharkskin suits and sequined evening gowns.

While the saxophone solos may be jumping off your turntables, James' first Motown bass lines are not always as easy to pick out. The miking and recording of bass guitars (and bass drums) was not in a highly evolved state in the late fifties and early sixties. To make matters worse, the fact that so many of Jamerson's first recording sessions at Motown were performed on upright bass makes his work even more difficult to discern. However, if you can manage to tune your senses in to the low end of some of these recordings, it will be well worth the effort. The next time that you listen to James' upright bass lines on a song like Marvin Gaye's "Can I Get a Witness," or Martha and the Vandellas' "Come and Get These Memories," try speeding up your record or tape. The bass will pop right out. You'll be amazed by what you hear (or what you haven't been hearing).

By the recording standards of today's digital world, the early Hitsville sessions were archaic, but they produced some of the warmest, fattest sounding recordings to ever grace a Chevy's dashboard speaker. Working with a used vintage 1939 Western Electric recording console, Motown's engineers had to cram all the musicians and singers onto just two tracks. In addition, lead and background vocals, horns, rhythm section, and percussion—everything, was cut live! There were no punch-ins. If you surmised that this procedure put a lot of pressure on James and the rest of the musicians, you win two Supremes' 45's. When someone made a mistake, everyone would have to go back to the beginning of the tune and start all over again. "We'd joke around and get on the guy who messed up," laughs Earl Van Dyke. "Then the guy who made the mistake would get an attitude like, 'OK, let's see who screws up this time.'"

Throughout it's early Detroit period, Motown obviously wanted to turn out the highest quality recordings possible, but the production team's attitude wasn't exactly as strict as the Berlin Philharmonic's Herbert Von Karajan when it came to precision. The logo on the purple and yellow Gordy records label proudly states, "It's what's in the grooves that count"—a philosophy that was devoutly followed by Berry Gordy and his producers. In Motown sessions, feel always superseded anything else that might have occurred on a given track. If the groove felt right, the producers just couldn't see scrapping an entire track and starting over just because someone had missed an accent or hit a wrong note. Besides, they figured that any listener who is petty enough to nitpick over a wrong chord or a misplaced rhythm while Marvin Gaye is pouring his guts out on a tune like "Hitch Hike," is probably missing the entire point of the record anyway.

Intonation problems during some of these sessions could not as easily be ignored. According to guitarist Joe Messina, "The intonation wasn't that good in the beginning. In fact, it was kinda nasty, but it got better as we went along because we became more aware of it." Most of the time though, poor ventilation was the culprit, as opposed to bad ears or shoddy tuning habits. The air conditioning and heating systems in Hitsville's studio added too much background noise to the recording process, so they were usually kept on during the rehearsals, and then turned off once the cutting started. With a dozen or more singers and musicians in the same small room, the climate, as well as the music being played, could heat up very quickly. To this day, Earl Van Dyke cannot listen to Marvin Gaye's "Try It Baby" without wincing in pain from the tuning problems. But hey, why don't you try and see if you can keep your guitar or horn in tune when the temperature is changing plus or minus fifteen degrees every half hour?

While Motown's early recording dates may not have been run in the same manner as a Nelson Riddle arranged Frank Sinatra session, the resulting hits were just as successful. The contrast in production philosophies doesn't negate the value of the finished musical product. In fact, it can be argued that the Motown sessions required more creativity on the part of the musicians and producers. "If you walked into a Nelson Riddle or Don Costa recording session," contends former Temptations and Supremes' music director, Gil Askey, "they'd have every note written out. In the early days of Motown, you'd be lucky to get a piece of paper with some chords scribbled on it."

The ingenious musical backgrounds that were recorded behind all of Motown's early stars were created through the exchange of ideas between the studio musicians and the producers. Motown was not yet ready for the more dominating role that arrangers began to take in highly orchestrated late sixties gems like "Love is Here and Now You're Gone" and "You're All I Need to Get By." This approach would have been out of place in the fresh sounding raw material of the early sixties. After a few years, the horn charts started to become more specific, but the arrangers' sparse treatment of the bass, keyboard, drums, and guitar charts would remain the same up until the late sixties. They preferred to allow enough room for James and the rest of the rhythm section players to do their thing. The attitude more or less being pursued was, "If it ain't broke, don't fix it." Besides, "the Motown Sound" was more a product of the heart than the pen.

WELCOME TO THE APOLLO

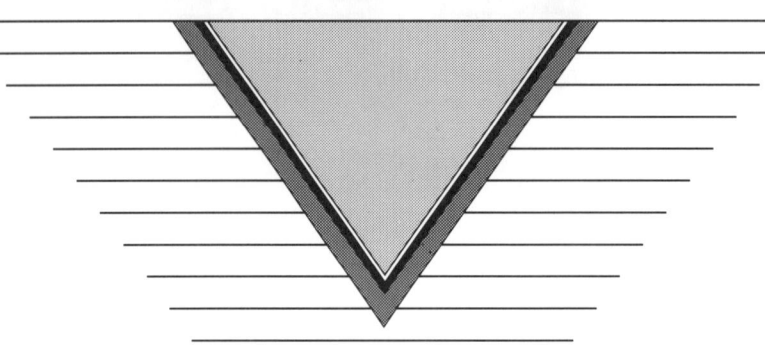

> *"Good evening ladies and gentlemen and welcome to the Apollo. We are now in the process of cutting a live performance—a very wonderful thing which we hope will go over real well, whereas, you can go out and buy your copy and say, 'Well, we were there that night.' So if you see things you like, help the artists along. You can stomp your feet, clap your hands, shake your head, just come on in and let them have a ball. Let's enjoy yourself, let your hair down, and if you can't let it down, take it off!! Right about now, I'd like to get moving in the swing of things by introducing to you a very talented group, and they're here just because they'd like to let you know that they can shake it on down. Ladies and gentlemen . . . the fabulous, Contours!!!"*
>
> -Bill Murray, M.C. for the Motor Town Revue-

Imagine going to a concert in a small intimate theatre and seeing the Temptations, the Supremes, Stevie Wonder, Marvin Gaye, the Miracles, the Marvelettes, and Mary Wells—all in one show! In today's over-inflated concert market where tickets routinely sell for twenty dollars or more, a lineup like this would command at least fifty bucks a pop (not to mention what the scalpers would charge). Well, it may sound impossible, but in the early and mid-sixties, Motown was regularly sending out revues just like this one, that could be seen for just two or three dollars. In the fall of 1962, when Berry Gordy sent out the first of these highly successful tours, which were called the Motor Town Revues, he had finally convinced the music industry that he and his new record company were a force to be reckoned with. For James Jamerson, this tour was the culmination of a three year period during which he had solidified his position as Motown's premier groovemaster.

The road was not exactly a new experience for James. Even before going out with Jackie Wilson, he had toured with all of the early Motown road shows in 1960 and 1961. These engagements were nowhere near the size or importance of the massive 45-member extravaganza that made up the first Motor Town Revue, but they had afforded Berry and his artists the opportunity to promote their records and get their feet wet in live venues. Traveling in a small caravan of cars to nearby Michigan locales like Flint, Idlewild, and Saginaw, the first road shows in 1960 were very well received, according to road bandleader Popcorn Wylie. "The live band at that time had Benny Benjamin, Mike Terry, myself, Jamerson, Eddie Willis on guitar, and Bob Cousar on trombone. We set attendance records all over the state."

James usually enjoyed the excitement of the road and the camaraderie of his fellow musicians. It was a time for him to stretch out musically, but it was also a period that provided the necessary breathing room for his volatile and sometimes eccentric personality. Describing the James Jamerson of this period, baritone player Mike Terry recalls:

"He was young, wild, and free. He was his own boss. I remember one time at a show in Idlewild, he got in the

middle of some argument between me and another guy. You see, he was like my big brother and he used to stick up for me. Anyway, it was kind of funny. All they did was circle each other in this room and mouth off from about four o'clock 'til six o'clock in the morning. Nothin' really happened."

One aspect of life on the road that James could never quite get used to was the traveling accommodations. Food was always one of his primary concerns. If Jamerson could find good home cooking style soulfood restaurants in the vicinity of the gigs, he considered the tour a success. Bad hotels and lousy food however, could occasionally make him difficult to be around. Bandleader Wylie remembers:

"We were on the road one time during the early days of Motown, and we were driving to a gig in my car with Hank Cosby, Marvin Gaye, who was drumming on a few dates, Mike Terry, myself, and Jamerson. It was about two or three o'clock in the morning and we were still traveling. Well Jamerson was just determined to get comfortable, so he puts on his hat and starts getting into his pajamas in this crowded car. After he had finished elbowing everybody changing out of his clothes and all, we finally figured that things had settled down, but then he starts eating from this smelly jar of pickled pigsfeet. To make matters worse, he lights up this big cigar and smoked up the car so bad that it was hard to see and drive. We were all in there close and the guys all started to fightin' and arguin' with him to cool it with the pigsfeet and the cigar. But hey, that was Jamerson."

Following the first road show, Popcorn left Motown to pursue his own career, and the new live road band turned out to be the same Joe Hunter band that had toured with Jackie Wilson. James' duties in this group were short lived however, because within a few months, Smokey Robinson snatched him up to become the Miracles' road bassist. Even though Berry's studio lineup was depleted whenever James and the rest of the musicians hit the road, Motown's 1961 production schedule was still flexible enough to hold up a recording session until they returned. Besides, most of the tours at that

Motown's first live orchestra in 1961. James is at the upper left corner playing the "Black Beauty" that was given to him by his friend, Chili Ruth. The drummer is Benny Benjamin, Popcorn Wylie is conducting, and the sax players from left to right are Hank Cosby, Mike Terry, and Bernie Peacock. The back row of horn players from left to right are Bob Cousar on trombone, and Russell Conway and "Little John" Wilson on trumpets.

time were fairly short and close to home, so recording delays were minimal.

By the fall of '62, Berry had armed himself with some serious ammunition to begin his assault on the theatres of the nation's "Chitlin' Circuit." With a string of hits under his arm like the Contour's "Do You Love Me?," the Miracles' "Shop Around," and the Marvelettes' "Please Mr. Postman" (which brought Motown its first #1 pop hit), Berry felt that the time was right for his performers to spread their wings and fly. Never one to shy away from delegating authority to qualified people, Berry placed the organization and planning of this project in the hands of his sister Esther and Thomas "Beans" Bowles, one of the reed players in the studio band. Creating a concept and coordinating the schedules for a traveling road show that included the Contours, Marv Johnson, the Supremes, Little Stevie Wonder, Mary Wells, the Marvelettes, Martha and the Vandellas, Singin' Sammy Ward, the Miracles, and Marvin Gaye was a monumental task, but by late October, they were ready. Berry packed his recording artists and musicians into an old bus and five cars, and the first Motor Town Revue pulled away from the curb at Hitsville. The tour opened on October 26 at Washington D.C.'s Howard Theatre, then made a brief swing through New England before taking on the Deep South, and finally ended up with a ten day run at the Mecca of R&B, New York's Apollo Theatre.

It took quite a bit of detective work to determine whether or not Jamerson went out with this tour. Esther Edwards, who is presently the director of the Motown Historical Museum in Detroit, told me that James' face is not included in the group photo that was taken in front of Hitsville just before everyone loaded onto the bus. But as baritone player Mike Terry points out, "That doesn't mean anything because there was a good chance James was off somewhere getting a 'taste' when the shot was taken." Mary Wilson, in her book *Dreamgirl*, remembers that James was on the first Revue because he was involved in a racial incident at a concert in Birmingham, Alabama. A moronic local security guard had taken offense to James' using a backstage bathroom that was supposed to be the exclusive property of whites.

Crowds would stand in line for hours to see Motor Town Revues like this mid-sixties show at Detroit's Fox Theatre. "Brigand of Kandahar?"

Still, most of the musicians that I interviewed could not verify whether or not he was a part of this tour, and the live album (*Recorded Live at The Apollo, Volume One*) that chronicles the first Revue is not much help either. The primitive early '60's live recording techniques make the bass sound like it was recorded in a high school gym, so it's almost impossible to tell who was playing. The most telling evidence is a photo (included in this chapter) that shows James onstage at the Apollo surrounded by a collage of Motown stars. The Apollo Theatre's marquee that is included in this collage lists all the names from the lineup of the first revue. In addition, the Miracles were on the bill, and from late '61 to early '64, they never performed without Jamerson.

The Motor Town Revues were much different from the early road shows that Popcorn Wylie and Joe Hunter took out. Berry had enlisted the services of a big band leader named Choker Campbell, who had been conducting and putting together the music for shows in Idlewild, Michigan's most popular black resort throughout the fifties and sixties. Choker and his band's influence on the musical arrangements, along with Beans Bowles' innovations on the presentation of the live shows were immediately felt. While the performances on *Recorded Live At The Apollo* may sound a bit stiff and unpolished, you can definitely see the direction in which Berry Gordy wanted his acts to head. Las Vegas and the Copa Cabana were beginning to loom on the horizon.

Two months later, in time for Christmas, Berry's entourage had returned home in triumph after having conquered the hearts and souls of audiences throughout the country. James' homecoming would be short-lived though. For much of the next two years, he would log thousands of miles with the Miracles in the United States, Canada, and the Caribbean. When the Miracles would join up with subsequent Motor Town Revues (later shortened to the Motown Revue), James would usually just play behind the Miracles, and road bassist Bobby Nicholson would handle most of the remaining acts on the show.

Beans Bowles and Smokey Robinson characterized the Jamerson of the roadwork years as "a hard partier" who got involved in too many arguments and fights for their tastes, but they both agreed that when it came time to play music, all of his extraneous dilemmas quickly dissolved. On stage, James exuded a quiet intensity. There was very little movement or showboating, yet anyone who knew him realized that he was on fire inside. You might occasionally see a smile break through his concentration, but that was about as far as it went. As Robert White recalls, "Every gig he ever went on, he came to play—and if you weren't ready to play, you weren't going to make it with Jamerson. He'd get right on you."

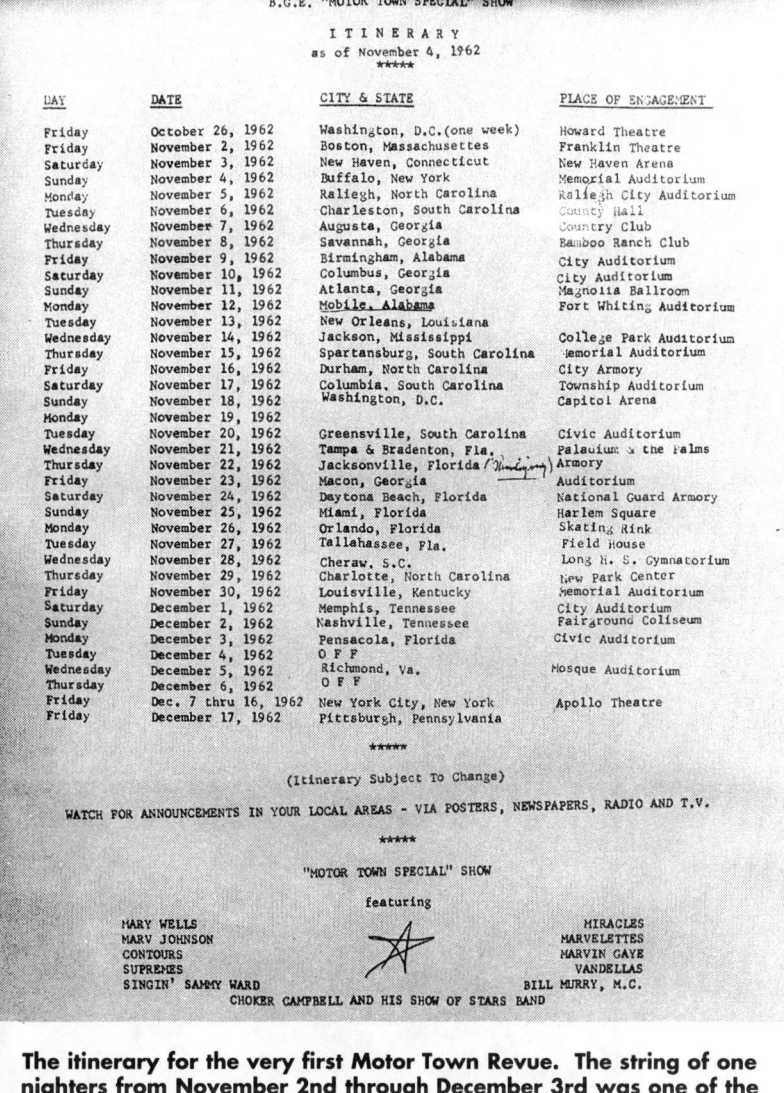

The itinerary for the very first Motor Town Revue. The string of one nighters from November 2nd through December 3rd was one of the most brutal tours in the history of Pop music. The school bus that the Revue traveled in was a far cry from the luxury tour buses of today.

By 1964, after almost four years of roadwork, everyone wanted James to come home. Things had gotten to the point where Motown would not record a track without him. Berry Gordy was growing tired of holding up sessions while he waited for James to finish up whatever Miracles tour he was on, and James' children were starting to wonder if they really had a father. "By that time, we had three kids, and James was away so much that they were saying, 'When is Daddy coming over?' instead of, 'When is Daddy coming home?'" says his wife Annie. "When Berry finally offered him two hundred and

Jamerson and the collage that was compiled for him during the 1962 Motor Town Revue. Clockwise after the marquee are MC Bill Murray, the Contours, the Supremes, Marvin Gaye, Little Stevie Wonder (with Bill Murray), Mary Wells, the Marvelettes, the Miracles, and bandleader-saxophonist Choker Campbell.

Jamerson on tour with the Miracles sometime during 1963. The center photo shows James, his wife Annie, Claudette Robinson, and Smokey Robinson.

fifty dollars a week to stay home, I convinced him that without the road expenses, he would make more at home than he would on the road, even though Smokey was paying him the same two fifty a week."

From this point on, Motown tried to keep their live and studio musicians separate. Guitarist Robert White explains, "Motown liked you to be in a category and put a label on you. For instance, they wanted the writers to be writers and the players to be players, and they also didn't want their road players doing studio work." (Although there were a few isolated exceptions like Miracles' guitarist Marv Tarplin and Temptations' guitarist Cornelius Grant.) Even on one of the rare instances when Earl Van Dyke and a few of the other studio players went out on the road to accompany the 1965 Tamla-Motown Revue in England, James was told to stay home because they wanted him to record some new tracks. He had just become too important to the sound that was emanating from Hitsville to be allowed to waste his abilities on the road. James would remain in the studio, imprisoned by his own talents, for the next eight years.

IGOR & THE FUNK BROTHERS

(PART ONE)

It is doubtful that James Jamerson would have reached the musical heights that he did without his fellow studio musicians at Motown. In Earl Van Dyke, Robert White, Benny Benjamin and the rest of the "basement residents" at 2648 West Grand Boulevard, James found his ultimate soulmates. They understood his tempestuous personality and his musical groove, and in them, he found the acceptance and trust that he had sought throughout much of his life. It was a match made in Rhythm and Blues Heaven.

From its earliest days, Motown constantly juggled its studio lineup in search of the perfect combination. By 1964, the evolution was complete; in a flurry of backbeats, tambourines, and red hot grooves, the Funk Brothers arrived on the scene and set the standard by which all future R&B rhythm sections would be judged. Keyboardist Earl Van Dyke credits drummer Benny Benjamin with the creation of the studio band's legendary title:

"The band that I was playing with in the clubs had Jamerson on bass, Robert White on guitar, and Uriel Jones on drums. Benny used to call us the Funk Brothers. By him coming up with the name, that made him Funk #1, but the name really applied to all the rhythm section players. Like the other two guitarists—Joe Messina and Eddie Willis, and the guys playing all the percussion, Eddie Bongo, Jack Ashford, and Jack Brokensha . . . they were all Funk Brothers too."

The Funk Brothers didn't only cut behind Motown's vocalists—and they didn't just cut for Motown. They also had a few instrumental albums of their own, but they were released under different names. Their 1963 LP entitled *Twistin' the World Around* was credited to the Twistin' Kings. Similarly, the recording artist's name used on their 1965 album, *That Motown Sound,* was Earl Van Dyke and the Soul Brothers. "Originally, we wanted to be called Earl Van Dyke and the Funk Brothers," says Earl, "but Berry said 'No, no, no!...,' he didn't want us to use that term. He felt that it wasn't appropriate so he changed it to the Soul Brothers. We didn't see the harm in the word because at the time, there were songs out like 'Funky Broadway' and Horace Silver's 'Opus de Funk.'" A few of the Funk Brothers non-Motown tracks that were cut during some of their "illegal" moonlighting

Joe Messina

Robert White

Eddie Willis

sessions were Jackie Wilson's "Higher and Higher," the San Remo Golden Strings' "Hungry for Love," and Edwin Starr's "Agent Double-O-Soul." There was also a Muscle Shoals session sandwiched in between all their Motown dates, but none of the musicians remember if the tracks were hits.

Earl Van Dyke was the unofficial leader of the Funk Brothers for a variety of reasons . . . dependability, musicianship, business sense, but most of all, he knew where to find the rest of the band members when it was time for a session. With the Funk Brothers, this was no small task. It required an intimate knowledge of Detroit's bar scene, particularly when it came to Jamerson and Benny. With James, it was usually a simple case of tracking him down at home or at one of his many favorite watering holes. According to Earl, Benny was another story entirely:

"A lot of times if we had a gig, you had to go and get Benny's drums out of the pawn shop. Over at the studio, they fired a night watchman one time because of Benny. He told the guy that we had a gig and he had to have the drums so Benny took the studio drums. The next day we came in for a session and the drums were supposed to be behind this baffle. Well, we wound up waiting for Benny to show up, so Jack Brokensha said that he would play the drums until Benny got there. But as soon as Jack went behind the baffle where the drums were supposed to be, he said, 'But where are the drums?' So I had to leave the session and find Benny.

"You see, Benny was really a jazz drummer but he was also a drug addict so he switched to R&B because it was easier to hold it together. When he was having trouble getting drugs, you just couldn't find him, or sometimes he would show up real late with some crazy excuse. Like one time, he said he got caught behind a truck on the highway that was carrying elephants for a circus that was in town. He told us the elephants got loose and blocked up the traffic, but we knew that was bullshit because Benny didn't drive."

Studio bandleader and keyboardist, Earl Van Dyke.

Wrecking Motown's production schedules was not the only thing that James and Benny had in common. They both had curious playing habits. Benny usually talked to himself while he played the drums, and James often sang a counterpoint to the tune while he was playing. (You would think that hearing David Ruffin or Levi Stubbs sing-ing five feet away would have been enough for him, but Jamerson had to get into the act.)

Oddly enough, there was very little musical interaction between Motown's stars and the studio musicians. Even though they cut together in the early days, Berry Gordy implemented a hands off policy that existed throughout Motown's Detroit period. "He didn't allow his artists to tell us anything," says Earl. "Producers . . . yes, but everyone else he kept away from us. We might hang out socially at company parties and stuff like that, but they could not tell us how to play." One notable exception actually worked in reverse. The Funk Brothers were expected to tell one of the artists how to play. Berry Gordy instructed them to teach music to Little Stevie Wonder for one hour every day. "When you hear Stevie play drums," says Earl, "you're hearing Benny Benjamin. He hung around us all the time." Often these music lessons degenerated into games of tag or hide-and-seek during which poor Little Stevie occasionally wound up getting locked in a closet by James, Benny, or one of his other "tutors."

According to Uriel Jones, Jamerson was usually center stage when it came to practical jokes and buffoonery. "We always had fun with Jamerson because there was usually something that he done did that we could talk about and laugh. We were always on him because he was the guy that always did everything." But while James' studio games were an important part of the morale and spirit of the Funk Brothers, these pranks also provide some of the most accurate insights into Jamerson's musical abilities.

Due to the legendary status that has grown around James' name amongst Detroit musicians, a simple question like "How good a sight reader was Jamerson?," can yield a response like, "He was such a mean sight reader that you could put a chart down on a music stand in South America and he could sight-read it from Detroit, backwards with a mirror, and get it perfect the first time." However, by recalling some of his studio escapades, Uriel Jones and Robert White were able to put things in perspective on the following Jamerson attributes:

On his speed in learning his parts during studio sessions . . .

"Jamerson learned his parts so fast sometimes that he would start clowning while the rest of us were still working out our stuff," says Uriel. *"He'd be playing a tune and stompin' his feet way out of time trying to mess us up. You couldn't look at him while he was doing it because it would throw you off. I had to turn my head. His coordination was amazing. He could be beating a waltz or a 5/4 pattern in a different tempo than the song we were playing, and still he'd never lose his groove."*

On his musical ear . . .

While some of the arrangers recall that Jamerson had a highly developed sense of relative pitch, Uriel insists that he had perfect pitch (the ability to hear any note and identify it out of thin air). "In the studio when you walked across the floor, the boards squeaked and Jamerson and Robert White would always be betting money on what that note was. I don't remember James ever being wrong—that's how good his pitch was. When he came to a session or a gig, he tuned his instrument up to itself just using his ear—no keyboard or nothin'."

On his sight reading ability . . .

"Jamerson was a great sight reader when he first came out of high school," says Robert White, *"but his skills atrophied from lack of use. Once his professional career took off, he was always asked to fake or interpret rather than read note-for-note. But he could still read really well when he had to. Sometimes when the Detroit Symphony came in to cut string parts, James would play his upright bass with their string section and he didn't seem to have any problems with those charts."*

The Funk Brothers L-O-V-E-D nicknames. For instance, Earl Van Dyke was dubbed "Chunk of Funk" because of his playing style and the 260 pounds that were behind his fingertips. And of course we can't forget percussionists Eddie "Bongo" Brown, Jack "White Jack" Brokensha, and Jack "Black Jack" Ashford—or guitarist Eddie "Soupbone" Willis, and drummer Richard "Pistol" Allen. (Under penalty of death or worse by the remaining Funk Brothers, I've been forbidden to reveal the nicknames for Robert White and Uriel Jones.) But by far, the most colorful nicknames belonged to the two guys with the most colorful personalities . . . Benny and James.

"Benny called himself Papa Zita," relates Earl Van Dyke. "He had everyone buffaloed into thinking that he was from Bimini, but he was really from somewhere down south in Louisiana." Pretty nuts huh?, but not nearly as weird as Jamerson's names. James wasn't content with just one name—he needed half a dozen. There was "The Hook" (named after the index finger of his right hand that plucked his strings—James was basically a one fingered player), "Funky Fingers," and a multitude of other equally creative names, but the one that most of the musicians remember is "Igor." Eddie Willis narrates, "James came to the studio one time with a bald head, and he looked like this guy on a TV cartoon. Somebody in the studio called him Igor and it just stuck. It was really strange seeing him with all his hair off."

Without a doubt, the most off-the-wall alias that James

gave himself was Diego Diegerson. He had been referring to himself by this name off and on since high school. For some odd reason, someone in his childhood had told him that he was Cuban. Jamerson, believing this fable, decided that if James in Spanish was Diego, then Jamerson must be Diegerson. "We all thought that was absolute bullshit," roars Robert White. "We knew that the two languages didn't use the same rules. Jamerson wouldn't translate to Diegerson. We just couldn't accept that." (James actually spelled the name Diegosa, but pronounced it Diegerson.)

As you can see, being a Funk Brother involved a lot more than just playing music. The band also functioned as a social club, an emotional support group, and an eating society. "We were always together doing something besides music," explains Uriel Jones. "We'd go horseback riding in Canada, or we'd be out boating on the Detroit River or Lake Erie in my cabin cruiser when we had the time. We partied and did a lot of things together. A lot of times after the gigs, we'd go to each other's houses just to eat and hang out."

As much as the assortment of drug and alcohol problems eventually destroyed the lives of some of its members, much of the Funk Brothers' closeness was a reaction to the problems stemming from their individual addictions and abuses. In the case of Jamerson, this relationship was essential. If not for the rest of the Funk Brothers looking out for him, he might have never had the chance to create the masterpieces that he did. "We really loved him but he was a case," points out Robert White. "I mean, he was a lot of responsibility. He was definitely a self destructive guy. We used to take turns handling Jamerson. One of the most famous funny lines in our band was, 'It's not my turn to take care of that mother fucker.' Taking care of him meant that we kept him straight on the job by keeping him away from liquor."

The brotherhood that existed in the studio tran-

James with drummer Uriel Jones in 1964 at a Detroit club called Blues Unlimited. (Dig the "Earl Van Dyke and his famous Motown recording band" logo on the drum head.) The small box plugged into the input of Jamerson's bass is an early wireless hookup. The box with the antenna on top of the piano is the receiver.

scended social status, ethnic backgrounds, and most of all—considering the tense atmosphere in mid-sixties Detroit—race. As Robert White continues, "When the riots were going on in '67, we used to tell Joe Messina, 'Don't worry Joe, we'll defend you.' We wouldn't let anybody hurt him because he was one of the guys, so we'd walk him to his car. We forgot that Joe was Italian. He was just a black guy with a white face. That's just the way we were. I've never felt more love in my musical career than when I was working at Motown with the Funk Brothers. I think that went for all of us."

IGOR & THE FUNK BROTHERS

(PART TWO)

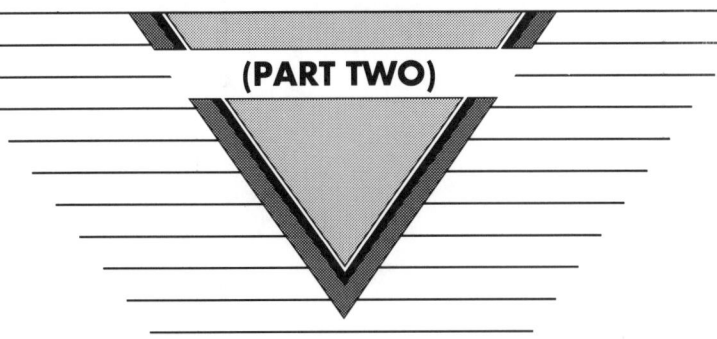

> "This is the room where it all happened. Earl Van Dyke used to sit over there at the grand piano, and behind that acoustic baffle over in the corner is where Benny Benjamin played his drums. And over here was where the singers would . . . . . ."

As Doris Holland shows visitors around the room, it becomes obvious to everyone that she takes great pride in her work. In her position as tour guide and administrative assistant at the Motown Historical Museum, she fully realizes the significance of the building in which she works. 2648 West Grand Boulevard is unlike any of the other family houses on the same block. Along with Abbey Road Studios, Graceland, and the old Fillmore East, the original home of Hitsville U.S.A. is one of the great shrines of popular music.

The tiny basement studio that is the focal point of the Motown Museum tour is silent now. The monitor speakers have been turned off for almost a decade and a half, but like the eerie feeling that permeates an old battlefield, this room too has its ghosts. If you close your eyes and concentrate, you can still hear Levi Stubbs pleading with Bernadette, or Diana Ross telling the world what her mama said . . . or James Jamerson, a cigar clenched between his teeth, playing his trademark eighth note introduction to "My Girl."

Today, the room is simply referred to as Studio "A," but back when the old Ampex tape recorder was still rolling, the Funk Brothers affectionately referred to it as "the Snakepit." What was it like to be in that room when those legendary sessions were being conducted? And what was the secret musical formula that so many other record companies and producers tried in vain to copy?

Earl Van Dyke is no longer the burly 260 pound "Chunk of Funk" that he was in the sixties. After Motown's exit from Detroit, and years of touring around the world with Freda Payne, Earl walks a little lighter and moves a bit slower, but his musical schedule remains as busy as ever. Today, instead of banging out block chords on Temptations tunes, his long supple fingers are more likely to be gently caressing the keys while playing through the changes of a song like Thelonius Monk's "Round Midnight." Now in his fifties, he has finally achieved his original goal in music—to make a living playing jazz in his hometown of Detroit. But he is very conscious of the impact that the Funk Brothers had on pop music during their earlier years.

It wasn't always that way, however. "A lot of the time, we thought the stuff we were playing was crap," says Earl. "None of us ever thought that Motown would get that big. It was just a gig to us. All we wanted to do was play jazz, but we all had families and at the time, playing rhythm and blues was the best way to pay the rent. Years later when you look back at all the stuff that happened . . . well, you see what it became."

The Mary Wells "My Guy" session was typical of the musicians' attitudes, and the manner in which their innate talents often triumphed over their dislike of some of the music. Earl, Jamerson, Benny, and the rest of the studio regulars had been recording all day long, and "My Guy" was the last tune that they were working on. With a half hour left in the session, the musicians had become bogged down in the intro section. As the time and their patience began to diminish, trombonist George Bohannon turned to Earl Van Dyke and said, "Hey Earl, the melody from 'Canadian Sunset' fits right over the chord changes of this intro." Earl, figuring one good theft deserves another, promptly added the left hand from Eddie Heywood's "Begin the Beguine" and Mary Wells had herself a classic intro. "We were doing anything to get the hell out of that studio," says Earl. "We knew that the producers didn't know nothin' about no 'Canadian Sunset' or 'Begin the Beguine.' We figured that the song would wind up in the trash can anyway." Earl was usually a pretty good judge of when a song looked like a hit, but not this time. "My Guy" went on to sell millions.

But don't get the impression that these musicians were just a collection of clock watchers who spent their entire careers plagiarizing their way into the top ten. In spite of their zany antics, the Funk Brothers were one of the most disciplined and creative hit machines of all time. Once they sat down to play, it was all business. With Motown constantly expecting them to crank out three to four songs during every three hour session, they must have been doing something right or they wouldn't have stuck around as long as they did. (An average work day consisted of 2 of these three hour sessions, and on occasion, as many as three or four.) Motown's producers and songwriters threw material at them at such a staggering rate that the musicians often had no idea what the songs were called, or who they were intended for. According to Earl, this constant work load occasionally led the Funk Brothers to seek refuge in unusual places when they wanted to escape the stressful atmosphere of the studio:

The home of the Motown Sound—"the Snakepit." The wide angle lens makes the room look larger than it actually is. The isolation booths were built into the wall on the right side.

"I remember when the producers would line up at the door so they could cut with us but you know, a lot of times we needed a breather. So what we would do was after we finished with one session, we'd always scatter. Like they had a little bar in the back that we used to hang out at behind the studio, and a couple of other bars up the street. But next door was Cole's funeral home, and sometimes James, Benny, and myself would go over there just to hide and drink. If the producers came and knocked on the door looking for us, we'd always send a

mortician to the door with his bloody rubber apron on and he'd go, 'No they're not in here,' but we'd be in there laughin' like mad because we knew that they weren't gonna' come in and find us."

The policies of the production and A&R departments had a great deal to do with the pressurized working conditions placed upon the musicians. Motown thrived on competition. In efforts to get recorded tracks past the scrutiny of Motown's quality control division, songwriters were pitted against songwriters, producers against producers, and even artists against other artists. But Brian Holland put the entire situation in perspective when he said, "It was a friendly kind of competition. There was a lot of pressure but it wasn't like some 9 to 5 office job or anything like that. It was fun man! We were making music with people we loved."

Fun or not, all of this creative energy eventually had to be dealt with by the Funk Brothers, and out of their efforts to handle all the material, a large part of Motown's hit making formula evolved. They didn't exactly turn to Bach, Beethoven, and Brahms for their musical role models in this pursuit. They found their system much closer to home . . . the assembly lines of Chrysler, Ford, and General Motors. Division of labor was the name of the game down in the Snakepit. Each of the musicians had specific roles that enabled them to lock in on their respective parts and cut finished tunes with a minimum amount of wasted motion.

The guitar section was the embodiment of this concept. With two or three guitarists playing on almost every recording date, an arranging system had to be devised so they wouldn't step on each other's toes. Earl Van Dyke playfully describes their approach to a typical Hitsville session:

"I used to call those guys Heckyll, Jeckyll, and Son because they were the talkinest guitar players I ever worked with in my life. When a producer would put down the arrangement, these three guys would sound just like a bunch of magpies talkin'. But what they were doing, if you gave them five minutes, was sorting out what they were going to do all the way through the tune."

The most common lineup that they arrived at had Joe Messina and his Fender Telecaster playing backbeats (short percussive chords that usually hit with the snare drum on beats two and four) and any difficult written parts. Eddie Willis, who favored a Gibson Firebird, was in charge of bluesy fills and funky rhythms, and Robert White rounded out the section by playing full bodied legato chords and strums. Motown's producers also liked to use Robert whenever they needed a distinctive tone on a melodic line, because of the sound that he got out of his Gibson L-5 and his thumbnail. "We all had our specialties, but all three of us actually played a little bit of everything," notes Joe Messina. "It all depended upon who the producer was or who grabbed the part first. As we were running it down, you might hear something and you'd play it, so it was your part."

The trio of drummers who played on Motown's sessions also had individualized assignments, but the reasons behind them were not always musical. Benny Benjamin was always the undisputed king of the drums down in the studio, but his erratic work habits caused the A&R department to look for someone who would study his style and act as a standby. They found the perfect man for the part in Uriel Jones. Jones wasn't fancy, but he provided a big steady beat that could be counted on 365 days a year, and best of all—he showed up on time!

If Benny had a musical flaw, it was his inability to play a good, consistent shuffle. Again Motown's casting department found the right man for the job in Pistol Allen, the master of the shuffle, and the only drummer in the world capable of cutting a perfect track while reading a racing form at the same time. Pistol's expertise can be heard on hits like "How Sweet It Is to Be Loved by You" and "Beauty's Only Skin Deep."

Just as Hitsville employed other drummers besides Benny Benjamin, Earl Van Dyke wasn't the only keyboardist at Motown. Johnny Griffith could often be found playing the Hammond organ while Earl played on the studio's four foot Steinway. On long sessions when Earl's hands became weary of pounding the ivories, Johnny and he would sometimes trade instruments in order to give Earl's hands the less strenuous job of playing sustained organ chords. Third keyboardist, James Gittens, who died tragically in a 1965 car crash, often doubled on vibes, but he is best remembered for his organ playing and glissando effect on "Stop! In the Name of Love."

Much of the instrumental color and drive that set the Motown Sound apart from all of the other sixties R&B labels was due to the inventiveness of the Funk Brothers' percussion section. There is a lot more happening in Motown tracks than just the standard tambourines and congas. Jack Ashford, Eddie Bongo, and Jack Brokensha would bang on anything if they thought it would help to produce a hit. How many pop tunes can you think of that start out with a bunch of guys stomping on plywood boards like in the intro to "Baby Love?" Or how about the galloping knee slaps in the Four Tops' "Reach Out I'll Be There?" It probably wouldn't have surprised anyone in the studio if the percussionists had pulled out a set of spoons, or a stick and a beer can.

But Black Jack, White Jack, and Bongo, also excelled on "normal" percussion instruments. Their ingenious use of vibes—an instrument that was common in jazz but was rarely used in R&B formats—had an important subliminal effect when played in unison with some of the other instruments. String lines on songs like "This Old Heart of Mine" began to shimmer, and Earl's ballsy piano voicings often took on a new textural dimension when Brokensha or Ashford doubled his parts in hits like "It's the Same Old Song."

So there you have it—all the individual elements that went into Motown's famed rhythm section sound . . . except for one. Where and how did James Jamerson fit into this cast of funketeers? Actually, he had the easiest role of all. He was just expected to be himself and weave his magic in and out of what everyone else was doing. It came to be expected that somewhere in a given tune, Joe Messina would probably play a backbeat, Jack Ashford would shake a tambourine, or Benny would play one of his patented drum pick-ups, but no one ever knew what James Jamerson would do—he was completely unpredictable.

The overwhelming solidity of Motown's beat liberated James from the necessity of constantly being a timekeeper. On a track like Stevie Wonder's "Uptight," in which Benny is pounding the snare drum into oblivion on every beat, Jack Ashford is playing quarter note tambourine, and Joe Messina is emphasizing beats two and four with his metronomic guitar backbeats, keeping time on the bass would have just been redundant. James was free to fly. However, he was also capable of playing with great subtlety and taste when the groove needed his support. One of the simplest and most elegant bass parts that he ever recorded occurred while Benny Benjamin's bass pedal was going wild in the Marvelettes' "Too Many Fish In the Sea."

However, the Motown Sound wasn't just based upon Benny, James, Earl, and a collection of individual hotshots playing their own grooves. There were also many important interactive roles between different members of the Funk Brothers. If Jamerson's bass line was written out and needed to be doubled by a guitar for tonal variation (as in Marvin Gaye and Tammi Terrell's "Your Precious Love"), Joe Messina would assume that job because he was the best reader. Likewise, when Earl's piano parts needed to be doubled, Robert White would take over. As Earl elaborates, "When Robert and I played parts in unison, we played so close and tight that a lot of times, they would stop the session in the middle of a tune and say, 'I can't hear the piano or I can't hear the guitar,' because they couldn't separate us—like on 'You Can't Hurry Love.'

"We had a lot of concepts," continues Earl. "With so many people playing chords, we all had to be very conscious of the registers that we played in. Otherwise, things started to get muddy. For instance, the guitarists used to divide up the neck so that one guy would play up high, one would be in the middle, and the third guy would play down low. The section sounded like one big chord voicing.

"A lot of my voicings depended on the type of tune we were working on. On most of the medium to fast tempo things, I played at the low end of the piano. For instance, an up tune like 'I'm Losing You' would be played at the bottom of the piano. Now when it came to the ballads, they always made me move up because they wanted me to do a lot of filling in—and we *always* tried to stay out of

James' register unless somebody was doubling him. Another concept was that we tried to keep the melody note of the vocalist from being the top note of our voicings. That way, we wouldn't detract from what they were singing."

Within all these rules and preconceived practices, it would seem that the musicians' creativity and input would be stifled, but the Funk Brothers just used the formula as a framework. As Earl attests, there was always plenty of room for them to interject their musical personalities and play off of each other's ideas and the ideas of the arrangers. "If there was something that Jamerson or someone else played that sounded good, then I'd pick up on it, or if there was something that I played that they liked, then they'd work off of what I did. We didn't talk that much. We communicated through music." Motown arranger and conductor Gil Askey adds, "Those guys were like a five or six man arranging team. They'd get into a song and you'd hear 'em say, 'Hey take this out; leave this in. I don't like that; leave that out. Try this here,' and so on. That's how it was done."

Producer Johnny Bristol illustrates how in tune the musical psyches of the Funk Brothers were when they were working in the studio:

"Sometimes during the sessions, James or Benny or one of the other guys would get up and go to the drug store, and you'd look around and say, 'Where is so and so?,' and they'd say, 'He'll be back in five minutes. He went to get a sandwich.' So we would start practicing without that person, and when they returned, it was as if they had been there all the time—those guys breathed together."

But while the Funk Brothers were grooving with each other, they weren't always connecting with the production staff. Egos were generally left outside of the studio, because both producers and musicians understood that teamwork meant hits . . . and hits meant money. Still, after working day in and day out in close quarters, some flare-ups were inevitable. It wasn't uncommon to see James, Earl, or one of the other musicians storm out of the studio

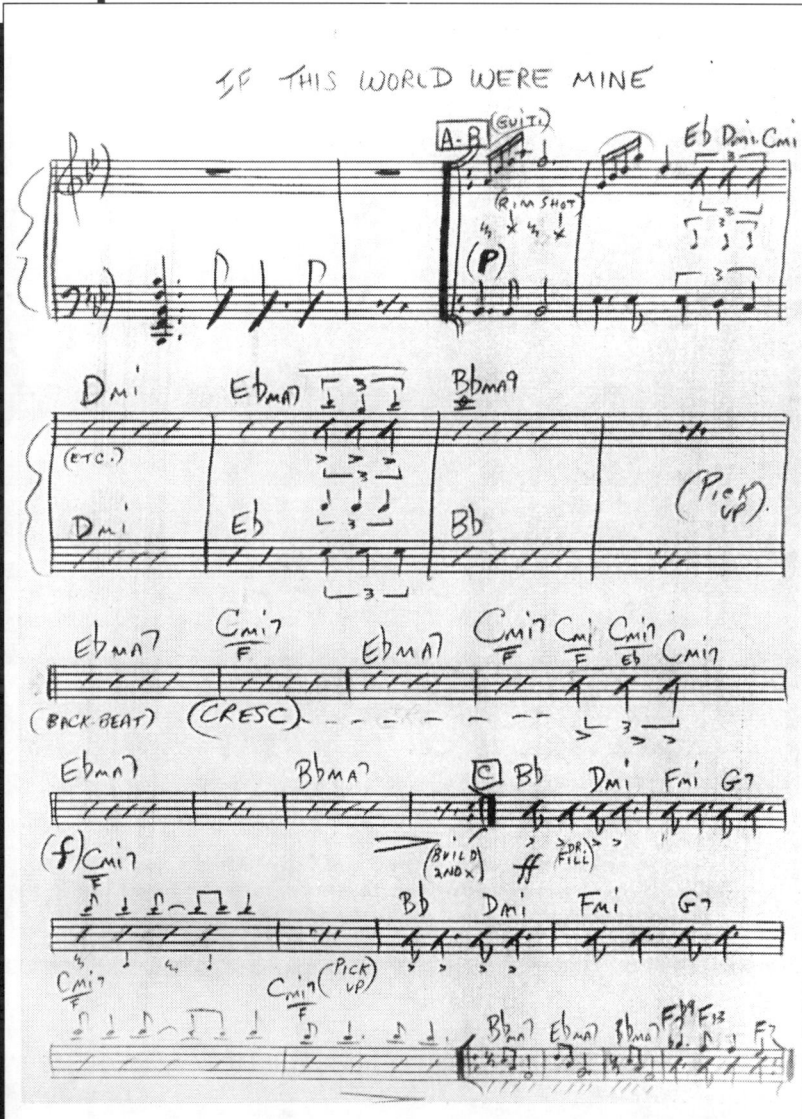

The original rhythm section chart that James and the Funk Brothers read from when they cut Marvin Gaye and Tammi Terrell's, "If This World Were Mine." This tune was recorded in 1967 during a period when the arrangers were beginning to write very specific lines for the studio musicians, but the chart is more indicative of some of the sparse chord arrangements of the early sixties.

The original rhythm section chart to Gladys Knight and the Pips' "I Heard it Through the Grapevine." This is a perfect illustration of how Motown's arrangers wrote for Jamerson in the late sixties. After giving a specific indication of the bass line throughout the first verse, the arranger then left it up to James to improvise off the basic groove.

in the middle of a session because of an argument with an arranger or producer.

One of the classic fights with the production staff occurred when the Funk Brothers played some quarter note triplets on an early studio date. "These guys had never heard a quarter note triplet before," remarks Earl. "They thought it was a mistake, so we had to convince them that what we were playing was just a common everyday rhythm." But according to Eddie Holland, the working relationship was generally very close and amiable once the musicians and production staff grew accustomed to each other's capabilities and habits. "James had a tendency to expose certain ignorances that some of the producers had in terms of their inability to read music," says Eddie. "But it was just his way of playing and teasing them. It was never hostile. Once he and the rest of the guys realized that we knew what we were doing, they respected us."

The amount of input and musical freedom that the Funk Brothers were allowed varied from producer to producer. Some, like Norman Whitfield, liked to have absolute control over every note that was played, while others, like Clarence Paul and George Gordy, practiced more of a hands-off policy that allowed the genius of the Funk Brothers to come forward. "George was cool," chuckles Earl. "He'd come in and say, 'OK fellas, I don't know nothin' about music, I don't know how to read music, and I can't play shit so you got it. Please give me a hit.' And he'd walk out. We'd see him in the control booth, but he wouldn't come down and bother us." "We'd work for him to the limit," adds Uriel Jones, "because he didn't have a big head and pretend like he knew something when he didn't."

"Another of our favorites was Clarence Paul," says Earl. "Clarence liked to cut late at night when we were at our worst, our drunkest, our highest ... whatever. One night we were working at the Chit Chat club and he came by to get us for a session. We didn't even get started until about a quarter-to-five because he took us out to get something to eat first. By that time, everybody was real drunk. I want you to know brother, we cut three tunes in thirty minutes! That's how much confidence the man had in us."

According to keyboardist Johnny Griffith, Holland-Dozier-Holland favored more of a teamwork approach when working with the Funks. "H-D-H had everybody come in to the studio at the same time like it was one big party. They'd give us four or five chords on a sheet of paper and we'd start studying and getting the feel of the tune. Brian Holland would walk around and whisper little patterns in your ear. With each player, he'd give one or two patterns to try and it would evolve from there."[1]

However, the party atmosphere of the Holland-Dozier-Holland sessions didn't apply to every studio date. Most hits were cut within forty-five minutes to an hour, but a few others involved marathon sessions that pushed the musicians to the limits of their musical skills and patience. Earl explains, "We were usually first or second take players, but some of the producers like Smokey Robinson and Norman Whitfield liked to do multiple takes in order to have a lot of material to choose from. On 'Tears of a Clown,' we did 44 or 45 takes. At least 40 of them were great, but Smokey was a perfectionist and there was something that he was looking for."

Jamerson wasn't quite as philosophical about it. "He hated doing a lot of takes," points out Robert White. "Usually after the 26th or 30th time through the tune, Jamerson would say, 'Rigor Mortis is setting in on this groove,' and sometimes he would refuse to play any more because 'rig' had set in. Young bassists have taken his records and played them not knowing what it really took to put them down on tape. For Jamerson, it might have been his twelfth great take. He seldom played the same thing twice. It still could sound the same but he'd change it somewhere."

As Hitsville vibist Jack Brokensha observes, Jamerson was often the barometer that let everyone know when to move on to the next song. "We'd make a few passes when they finally got the tune together, but when Jamerson stood up at the end of the fade, *that* was the take. *That* was the sign of approval."

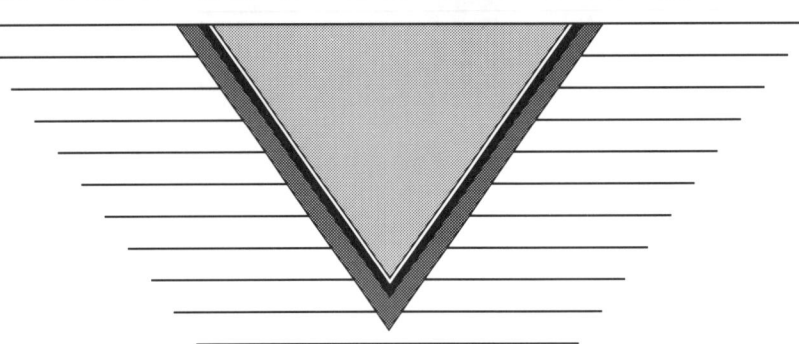

WE'RE IN THE MONEY

Hitsville must have seemed like a safe harbor in the troubled seas of the the mid-sixties. America was still reeling from the shock of Kennedy's assassination, and civil rights marchers were routinely being tear gassed and arrested in the South. With frightening regularity, more and more U.S. troops were being sent off to fight in Vietnam, and Dr. Richard Kimball, *the Fugitive*, still hadn't caught the one-armed man—but down in the Snakepit, things couldn't be groovier.

The Supremes were on a tear. From 1964 to 1965, they charted five consecutive #1 pop hits with "Where Did Our Love Go," "Baby Love," "Come See About Me," "Stop! In the Name of Love," and "Back In My Arms Again." Right on their heels were major scores by the Temptations and the Four Tops with "My Girl" and "It's the Same Old Song," and before you could say "Shotgun," the entire company was on fire—everyone was cranking out the hits. "There was something happening here that had never happened before," says producer-songwriter Johnny Bristol. "There was a busy recording studio where musicians, writers, artists, executives, and office people could all make money, and it was a growing thing. There was an enthusiasm there that would make any creative individual want to do his best. The creative flow went all the way through the company, from the shipping department to the front office."

The affluence that resulted from Motown's overnight success was not restricted to only Berry Gordy and his stars. The wealth that the company was beginning to enjoy was starting to trickle down to the Funk Brothers. Many of the musicians were now under contract to Motown, and the union scale of $52.50 per three hour session now became the norm. In addition, the overtime scales of $52.50 for the next hour and a half, and $52.50 for each subsequent half hour also went into effect. While this may not exactly sound like big time money, it tended to add up very quickly. Don't forget, the Funk Brothers were generally working two or three sessions a day, six days a week. By the mid-to-late sixties, they were probably some of the highest paid studio musicians in the country.

"In 1966, I made $100,000, and Jamerson and everybody else was making good bread too," declares Earl Van Dyke. "You see, Berry was easy to talk to. He never really mistreated us. Every time we would scream about money, we didn't have any problems because he would just say, 'Hey man, ain't no big thing. Ain't nothin' but some money,' and he would give it to us. The thing was, we just didn't know what to ask for. But still, I was knocked out to be getting a thousand dollars a week, fifty two weeks a year plus bonuses, and that didn't even include what I made on my evening gigs. We all had homes, cars, boats, horses . . . if you didn't come out of Motown with some money, it wasn't Berry's fault. Look at Joe Messina. He invested the money he made with Motown in a chain of car washes and now he doesn't even have to work unless he wants to. He ain't doin' nothin' but hanging out on his back porch eatin' snails."

However, not all of the musicians at Motown recieved the same treatment, and consequently, not everyone shares Earl's positive outlook. With all the revenue flowing into Hitsville, some people felt that they deserved more than they were getting. In addition, it didn't sit too well with some of the musicians that Motown began enforcing its ban on outside studio work. Berry Gordy had nurtured Motown's million dollar sound and he intended to keep it his sole property. When James and some of Hitsville's other studio aces would occasionally travel across town to cut at other studios like Ed Wingate's Golden World, someone from Motown's front office would be waiting at the door to slap them with fines.

But Robert White protests, "You know, I think too much is put on Motown's negative aspects. Motown had a lot of positive aspects too. There were some very groovy lifestyles that were appreciated by people who wouldn't have had them if not for Motown's generosity. They never say how many times Motown has gotten people out of jail or kept the court off their butts. Motown did me a lot of good. I mean, my first house that I ever had in my life I bought because of the salary that Motown paid me."

Most of the people on Motown's payroll were young street kids who had never dreamed of the kind of wages that they were now earning. Trying to look out for their welfare, Berry Gordy brought in a financial consultant to instruct his disciples on how to invest their money. And do you know what? It worked! Everybody promptly went out and invested . . . in Cadillacs. West Grand Boulevard began to look like a showroom at a General Motors dealership. "We looked up one day and Joe Messina drives up with this big Eldorado," laughs Earl Van Dyke. "We all said, 'Hey, wait a minute Joe,' and he says, 'Well, I might as well get with the rest of my black brothers.'"

James was right in there with the rest of his buddies too. He loved big old Buicks and Caddys. He also liked to have them cared for, so every time he played the Twenty Grand club on the west side of Detroit, he would pay the doorman $125 a week to park his wheels and look after them. Years later when Annie found out about these extravagances, she understandably hit the roof. It's too bad that James didn't care for his automobiles as well as the doorman did, because he cracked up quite a few of them. The fast lifestyle that he was beginning to lead also applied to his driving habits. It didn't matter though. When he totaled them, he just bought some more.

James actually wasn't really as irresponsible as this may make him appear. The welfare of his family always took precedence over any toys he may have wanted to buy for himself. The initial $250 a week that Berry Gordy had offered James when he came off the road was immediately put to good use. As soon as his Miracles commitments were through, he quickly moved Annie and the kids into a three bedroom house that he had purchased on Detroit's West Side. At a 1965 birthday party for James, Berry Gordy stopped by and saw the new house for the first time. Annie recalls Berry being extremely proud and excited that the business he had created was affecting the lives of his company workers in such a positive manner. "When Berry walked through the door, he looked around and said, 'Man if this is the way Jamerson is spending his money, I don't mind paying him.'"

Financial fortune was not the only "art form" flowering down in the studio. Music was still the number one priority at Motown, and the well of creativity seemed bottomless. The talents of the artists, musicians, songwriters, and producers seemed to be growing almost as

Judging by the facial expressions of Jamerson and Uriel Jones, there was either a very serious groove going on at the time this photo was taken, or a fight was just about to break out in the club.

quickly as their egos. "No one could tell us that we weren't the greatest players in the world," reminisces Robert White. "We played the Twenty Grand and the rest of the clubs just for partying money. We didn't really need it and we'd usually spend the evening's pay at the club before we even made it. We made that much in one hour in the studio." Keyboardist Johnny Griffith boasts,

"You could compare our rhythm section to anything else happening at that time and we were just better. The Motown thing was so much tighter. When we locked into a groove, it was hellacious."[2]

One element of the Motown scene that was definitely growing faster than both egos and money combined was James Jamerson's bass playing abilities. Through 1965, James probably had the funkiest and most melodic eighth note bass style in the universe, but for some reason toward the end of the year, he exploded in a completely new direction. Sixteenth notes, quarter note triplets, open string techniques, dissonant non-harmonic pitches, and syncopations off the sixteenth seemed to enter into his style almost overnight. It closely paralleled the change in the jazz world from Charlie Parker's eighth note bebop style to the evolution of John Coltrane's sixteenth note "sheets of sound" approach. There is a distinct break from the bass lines Jamerson was playing in '64 and early '65 on tunes like "Dancing in the Street" and "Stop! In the Name of Love" to '66 and '67 masterpieces like "Reach Out" and "I'm Wondering." Out of nowhere, James started playing almost as if he was the featured soloist. Even more amazing was his ability to play extremely busy bass lines without getting in the way of the vocalists.

Fortunately, Motown's producers and the rest of the Funk Brothers were open-minded enough to recognize his genius and allow him the space that was necessary for him to do his thing. In the midst of their established hit-making formula, Motown always encouraged experimentation. Other less creative musicians and record companies would probably have smothered Jamerson's newly inspired concept.

James' dramatic musical flowering was as much a part of Motown's new prosperity as it was a natural progression of his own innate talents. The infectious smell of success that permeated West Grand Boulevard was attracting a lot more than just salesmen pushing beehive wigs and evening gowns for the Supremes. Gifted arrangers like Paul Riser, Wade Marcus, Gil Askey, David Van DePitte, and in particular, songwriter-arranger Valerie Simpson and her lyricist husband Nick Ashford were joining the company and discovering that the musical happenings down in Studio "A" were the perfect outlet for their creative energies. The level of harmonic and melodic depth that they brought with them had been absent in earlier Motown productions. The basic triadic and seventh chord style of tunes like "Hitchike" and "Do You Love Me?" was now being replaced by sophisticated chord substitution techniques, upper partials and altered chords, and lots of inversions and pedal points. Some of the brilliant Paul Riser-Ashford-Simpson collaborations like "Ain't No Mountain High Enough" pushed the musicians to their limits. "I was afraid of Valerie Simpson's sessions," reflects Joe Messina. "They were really difficult. She was a very talented lady."

The musical sophistication that some of these new writers and arrangers introduced at Motown was just what James Jamerson needed to realize his potential. Robert White narrates, "Jamerson was at his best when he had a real bitchin' part to read. He would read it like no one else could read it. He was a lot more disciplined than some people give him credit for. In fact, he looked for an opportunity to be disciplined. When you gave him a completely free hand, sometimes he couldn't deal with that because he wanted to play everything he had ever learned in that one tune. That's when he became undisciplined. With Valerie Simpson's arrangements, he would try to put more into it and she would say, 'No, not this time buddy. I want those actual notes.' He'd still slip two or three in that she might like or let go. He was crafty."

The sources of Jamerson's musical inspiration were as varied as his bass lines. In an interview with *Billboard's* Nelson George, James talked about some of the origins of his ideas:

"My feel was always an Eastern feel, a spiritual thing. Take 'Standing In the Shadows of Love.' The bass line has an Arabic feel. I've been around a whole lot of people from the East, from China, and Japan. Then I studied the African, Cuban, and Indian scales. I brought all that with me to Motown."[3]

Sometimes, the strong influence of "the street" took precedence over the etherial vibrations and esoteric approaches used in songs like "Standing In the Shadows of Love." Jamerson continues:

I picked up things from listening to people speak, the intonation of their voices; I could capture a line. I look at people walking and get a beat from their movement ... There was one of them heavy, funky tunes the Temptations did ... I can't remember the name, but there was this big fat woman walking around. She couldn't keep still. I wrote it by watching her move."[4]

Drummer James Gadson and bassist Ron Brown, two of Jamerson's Los Angeles friends, had similar conversations with him. Gadson recalls, "I asked Jamerson what he was thinking about when he played 'Bernadette,' and he told me, 'I was dreaming that I was in the desert riding a camel.'" Ron Brown remembers one occasion during which he asked Jamerson where his ideas came from: "He told me 'Sometimes, I'd just look at a flower and the way it would sway would make me feel like playing a cer-

The original rhythm chart to Smokey Robinson and the Miracles' "I Second That Emotion." Comparing Jamerson's recorded lines to the parts written for him by Motown's arrangers affords a rare look into his creative thought patterns, and the manner in which he interpreted musical arrangements.

tain way, or I'd hear a car go down the street and hear something.' Everything had a musical orientation to him," interprets Brown. "He could transpose it into a musical result."

Jamerson was also inspired by more mundane occurrences—particularly the technological ones. When the increased revenues that were flowing into Hitsville permitted Mike McClain to make a dramatic upgrade of the recording facilities, James went to town. Beans Bowles explains, "The advent of better recording made him play busier because now he could be heard. His bass wasn't lost in the background like on some of the early recordings." Gil Askey adds, "When they went to eight track, they always tried to keep Jamerson alone on a track all by himself so that other instruments wouldn't get in the way of what he was doing. They knew where their sound was."

A late sixties club gig with Eddie "Bongo" Brown, Uriel Jones, and James, playing at a Detroit nightspot called Ben's High Chapparal.

However, not everyone appreciated the "busier style" that Beans Bowles described. The road bassists in particular were not exactly jumping for joy every time a new track like "I Was Made To Love Her" or "I Heard It Through the Grapevine" was released. They held James in the highest regard, but they also had the unenviable task of trying to re-create his bass lines on stage. Annie remembers James coming home from the studio one day and grumbling that he had been told to simplify his bass playing a little bit because the music on the road shows was suffering. "They told him that no one could play his bass parts," explains Annie.

By 1965, Hitsville's producers wanted to make sure that they could have Jamerson's services any time they needed them, so James was placed on retainer. He also started to recieve preferential treatment, but as Robert White observes, it was not undeserved. "He was favored over all of us. I don't think that there was a musician who felt that they were on an even par with Jamerson when it came to dealing with the front office. He had contributed more to his instrument than any of us had contributed to ours as far as the industry was concerned."

Robert hit the matter right on the nose. Of all the Funk Brothers, James was the most difficult musician for Motown's front office to deal with, but the personnel and musical situation demanded that he be treated in a different manner than the rest of his buddies. It was simple logistics: Uriel Jones or Pistol Allen could usually cover for Benny. There were three guitar players so the loss of one of them wouldn't have been devastating, and even Earl Van Dyke could be spelled by Johnny Griffith or James Gittens when the occasion demanded it... but there was only one James Jamerson.

STOMPIN' AT THE CHIT CHAT

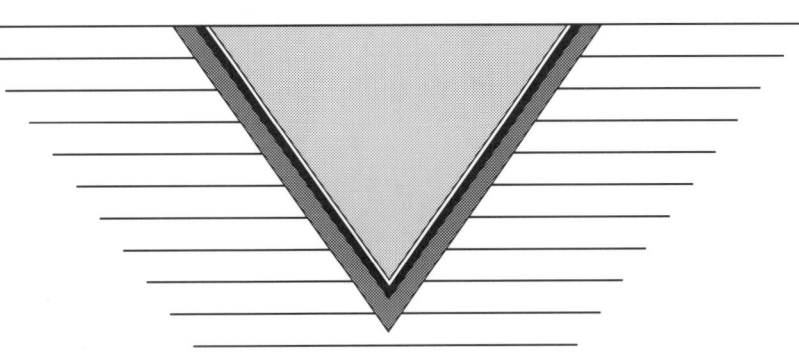

James Jamerson and the rest of the Funk Brothers were throwbacks to a different era and a different musical lifestyle. If you chased around after Thelonius Monk or Bird and Dizzy during New York's jazz scene of the late thirties and early forties, you could watch them play all day in recording studios and rehearsal halls, and then catch them jamming all night at Harlem clubs like Minton's, Clark Monroe's Uptown, or Dan Wall's Chili House. The Funk Brothers followed the same script, except the location was the west side of Detroit, and the clubs were called the Chit Chat, Blues Unlimited, the High Chaparral, and the Twenty Grand.

Earl Van Dyke remembers, "We were the house band at a lot of different clubs around town, but our home base was the Chit Chat. The band would usually be Robert White on guitar, Jamerson, myself on Hammond organ, Dan Turner or Lefty Edwards would play sax, and Uriel Jones or sometimes Pistol would play drums. We used to use Benny but we stopped because he was too unreliable. You never knew if he was going to show up. The pay wasn't a lot. Maybe fifty or sixty dollars a night per man, but we didn't really do it for the money. You see, all the guys were jazz musicians. I had played with Charlie Parker and Sonny Stitt, Benny had been with Dizzy Gillespie, and Jamerson gigged with Grant Green and Yusef Lateef. Jazz was our first love. The reason we worked at night was to take out all our musical frustrations from playing all that shit during the day in the studio. We'd record all day, go home, eat, and be at the club from nine to two, and then we'd have to be back in the studio again in the early morning. Sometimes, we would even go back to the studio after the club and we would stay all night doin' another session."

"The Motown Sound" benefitted a great deal from these club dates. Much of the chemistry and electricity that the Funk Brothers were able to generate in the studio was a by-product of the thousands of hours that they spent playing together at night. In the clubs, there were no time clocks or producers, so there was plenty of room for experimentation. Many of the grooves that made it to vinyl over at Hitsville actually had their origins in Chit Chat jam sessions. A longtime favorite among the club's audiences was a Funk Brothers' original called "The Flick," which was co-written by Earl, Jamerson, and Robert White. At Motown, James didn't get much of a chance to solo, but at the Chit Chat, it was a completely different story. He could stretch out as much as he wanted to, and "The Flick" was usually the song on which he would cut loose. (If you're ever lucky enough to come

The Funk Brothers posing at the Chit Chat club in the mid-sixties. From left to right: Robert White, Dan Turner, Earl Van Dyke, Uriel Jones, Jamerson, and Detroit radio personality, Martha Jean "The Queen" Steinberg.

41

Jamerson playing his upright at a Detroit club gig with Johnny Griffith on keyboard and Pistol Allen on drums.

James and Pistol performing at the Twenty Grand with blues singer, Joe Williams.

across a copy of Earl Van Dyke's *"Earl of Funk"* LP, cue up to the album version of "The Flick" and you'll hear an extremely "bad-ass" bass solo.)

Martha Jean "The Queen" Steinberg is presently vice president and general manager of WQBH in Detroit where she broadcasts her daily "Inspiration Time Gospel Program," but in the sixties, she had a blues show on WJLB that used to air some of the Funk Brothers' performances at the Chit Chat. She recreates a typical evening at the club:

"They didn't call themselves the Funk Brothers at the club. When I MC'd the shows, I would introduce them as Earl Van Dyke's band, and then I would introduce each of them separately and make comments on each musician. They would play all kinds of stuff: blues, jazz, rhythm and blues, and sometimes they might back up a local singer or recording star. We had a lot of musicians coming in to check out the band, and Jamerson in particular. They knew what he was doing around the town. He was very respected."

Playing in clubs was more than just a musical outlet for Jamerson. It was also a safety valve that allowed him to let off some steam after the daily stress that he had to contend with in the studio. As Uriel Jones laughingly illustrates, sometimes the valve was wide open:

"He was always full of shit, but he was always straight enough to play in the studio. Now on the night gigs though, he'd get tore up sometimes where we'd have to pull the plug on him. We'd just unplug his amp. Then he'd be so embarrassed that he wouldn't get off the stage. He'd still be up there fakin' like he was playing, so Earl would have to cover the bass on the B3 organ.

"I remember one night at the Chit Chat, there was a birthday party for Martha Jean and we made him get off the stand. Martha Jean kept saying to us, 'Why did you do that to Jamerson? Don't do Jamerson like that.' Meanwhile, James went back around to the dressing room where we had hid Martha Jean's cake, and all of a sudden, we heard this big crash. Jamerson comes stumbling back out of the room with cake all over him everywhere . . . I mean, all over his face and everything. He went back there and fell in the cake. Martha Jean was just outdone. That was one of the nights that we pulled the plug." (Martha Jean is a woman of deep moral and religious conviction, but even she had to chuckle recalling that incident.)

The Funk Brothers were also regulars at the Twenty Grand, a 300 seat club that featured recording acts like

Vocalist Wendell Wells singing with the world's greatest club band. From left to right: Robert White, Earl Van Dyke (obscured by Wells), James Jamerson, and Uriel Jones.

Joe Williams, Harold Melvin and the Bluenotes, plus Motown stars like Marvin Gaye, the Spinners, and Martha and the Vandellas. James usually tried to keep his professional and family life separate, but he couldn't resist showing off for his wife and kids at the club's

A 1964 shot of the Funk Brothers playing a party at Blues Unlimited for Motown producer, Ivy Hunter. Ivy is on vocals, Jamerson is grooving in front of his Ampeg B-15, Dan Turner is the tenor player, Earl Van Dyke is on the Hammond organ, and Robert White is the guitarist.

You never knew who might show up when the Funk Brothers were jammin'. At the same party for Ivy Hunter, a few friends stopped by to help him celebrate. From left to right: Levi Stubbs, Dan Turner on sax, Ivy Hunter, Jamerson, Stevie Wonder, and Marvin Gaye.

Saturday matinees. Annie recalls, "We'd be driving home after he finished playing and he would always ask me, 'How did I sound baby?,' and I'd laugh and say, 'James, you know you always sound good.' The whole band sounded great all the time, unless they didn't like the act that they were backing up. If James and the rest of the guys liked the performer, they would make him sound like a million dollars, but if someone came in with an attitude, they would try to mess them up."

Jamerson always had a history of run-ins with club owners, but his dispute with the proprietor of the Twenty Grand was a classic. Earl Van Dyke narrates:

"The owner of the Twenty Grand was this Lebanese guy named Bill Kabash. One night, he comes up to us after we had finished playing with Marvin Gaye, and he says, 'Listen fellas, Wayne Cochran and the CC Riders were here earlier this week and they were some of the most polite white southern boys you would ever want to meet. They were calling me Mister Bill, and I don't see why you guys shouldn't call me that too.' Well, when Jamerson heard this, he flipped out and said, 'Mr. Bill? Mr, Bill my ass. You can go *!%&*!,' and then we all went off on him. He should have known that there ain't no way that was ever gonna' happen with us."

Even though the majority of his club work usually involved Earl, Robert, and Uriel, Jamerson still played live engagements with other musicians and band leaders. Sometimes he would pick up a theatre gig or a nightclub job playing behind someone like Tony Bennett or Shirley Bassey, just so he could get in some playing time on his upright. He had a tendency to completely over-extend himself with live engagements—not so much for the love of money—but for the love of playing the bass. It was a very strong addiction. Eddie Willis recalls one evening that illustrates just how deep this addiction was:

"Me and James would play in clubs sometimes with a blues harmonica player from Detroit who was named Little Sonny. We'd play songs like "Got My Mojo Workin'," "You Got Me Runnin, You Got Me Hidin',"... y'know, standard blues tunes. Well I remember on one of these gigs, James smashed his hand in a car door on the way to the club, and he spent the whole night playing with blood dripping from his hand. He should have gone to the hospital, but instead he played the gig. If he wanted to play, nothin' would stop him."

DON'T MESS WITH JAMES

After a five year hiatus from live performing, Marvin Gaye returned to the stage for an historic concert at the Oakland Coliseum on January 4, 1974. As Marvin plunged into "Trouble Man" for the opening number, the sellout crowd barely noticed that one of his background musicians was tearing the roof off the arena with his bass playing . . . after all, it was Marvin's night. Almost a decade and a half later, the *Marvin Gaye Live* album that resulted from that concert has a haunting quality about it. After the introduction and overture, as Marvin begins to croon, "I come apart babe, but that's okay, I'm a trouble man, don't get in my way," you can't help but feel that, to a certain extent, it was autobiographical. But Marvin wasn't the only troubled soul on stage that night. His lyrics were also a fitting commentary on a side of the life of his bassist, James Jamerson.

James didn't go looking for problems but in his environment, they had a way of finding him. It's not exactly a classified state secret that Detroit does not place in the annual top ten list of safest American cities. The Motor City has always been a tough town, but probably never more so than in the racially polarized atmosphere of the late sixties. Whether you were black or white, finding yourself in the wrong neighborhood at the wrong time could be dangerous to your health. Detroit musicians who walked out of clubs after their gigs at two or three o'clock in the morning were prime targets, because everyone knew that they had cash and instruments. Introduce to this scenario one budding young musical genius with a short fuse, and you have the potential for some explosive situations.

Jamerson's notorious temper and unpredictability caused some people around Motown to give him a wide berth. His five foot, seven inch stature belied his hell-raising ability. However, as James Jr. points out, "My Dad just didn't like to be pushed around. As long as you didn't mess around with his family, his music, or his money, it was easy to get along with him." Still, James enjoyed his "tough guy" image. A large measure of his reputation stemmed from bravado, but when provoked, he could become very nasty in a hurry. Just ask some of the club owners who were foolish enough to try and pull a fast one when it came time to pay James at the end of an evening of playing. They'd usually see things his way after about a dozen bottles of liquor were smashed on the floor.

Occasionally though, Jamerson would bite off more than he could chew. One night after a long evening of playing at a club, he had to make a telephone call in the phone booth outside. The booth was occupied for quite some time and James began to get impatient. When his requests to the occupant changed over a period of time from, "Are you going to be long?," to banging on the door and screaming, "Get the hell out of there!," the besieged caller eventually flashed his police badge and beat the hell out of James.

It was quite common in the sixties for Detroit club musicians to carry guns for protection and James was no exception. This practice got him into trouble sometimes, but guitarist Dennis Coffey recalled one occasion when it paid off:

"We had been recording all day and James and I decided to have a drink and talk a little while before we went home to our families. As we were walking to a bar, this guy holds us up at gunpoint and tells Jamerson to empty his pockets. Well, Jamerson used to carry this one-shot .22 caliber Italian gun that looked like a

pen. I guess the mugger didn't know what it was because when James emptied his pockets, the mugger just took the wallet and started to walk away. All of a sudden, James chases after the guy who didn't expect this at all, and he sticks this little gun in the guy's neck and says, 'Give me back my wallet.' When he gave Jamerson back his wallet, James said, 'Now give me your wallet.' He wound up mugging the mugger."

At this point, this is probably beginning to sound like the story of "Dirty Harry" Jamerson, but the non-musical side of James' reputation actually owed more to martial arts expert Bruce Lee than to gunslinger Clint Eastwood. His lifelong passion for karate was more for show than for actual use on live targets. Nevertheless, he was almost as proud of his martial arts abilities as he was of his bass playing. West Coast studio guitarist David T. Walker recalls James boasting from time to time that "he could pull somebody's heart out" if he became involved in a life threatening situation.

Luckily for Detroit, James limited his martial arts expertise to his karate class or his backyard, where his family occasionally saw him breaking bricks and boards with his head, hands, and feet. The City of Chicago was not so fortunate. On one rare occassion when Motown sent him out for a late sixties road show, James' temper got the best of him when he became incensed with an arrogant desk clerk at his hotel. He had locked himself out of his room and the clerk refused to give him a key, insisting that he wasn't James Jamerson. When Motown promotions director Weldon MacDougal came to the front desk and finally straightened things out, Jamerson, without warning, leapt over the counter and knocked out the bewildered employee with a karate chop.

The Karate Men: James and his buddies from martial arts class. The tall mean looking guy in the center is his teacher, Mr. Hotse.

Despite all these stories, not everyone looked at James as the sixites answer to "the Terminator." Robert White narrates:

"He wasn't that tough but he was durable. You couldn't hurt him. He was one of those guys that, you could beat his ass real good and he'd just get up and walk away. He actually got in more arguments than actual fights. James would bluff because he knew about his feet. He couldn't run so the best thing for him to do was to stand there and woof and hope that he could scare you off because if he had to flee the scene, it was his ass.

"He had a weird karate style. I remember one time I really wanted to see him perform because he looked like he knew something. I thought that it would be a good thing if he came down to my dojo (karate school) one day when we had two schools fighting each other and comparing Japa-

nese and Korean styles. Anyway, he wouldn't take off his damn socks because he was embarrassed about his feet, so they wouldn't let him out on the floor. He could have hurt himself for lack of traction. Maybe a week later after this thing was over, he had gone around telling everybody that he had kicked my ass. This was really funny because sometimes, Jamerson could be a habitual liar in a comical sort of way. It was part of that acceptance thing. He always wanted to be bigger than life. So everybody said to me, 'Did he really kick your ass?,' and I said, 'Yes he did. Man, I didn't even have a chance.' I said that right there in front of him, and he looked at me all weird you know, because he didn't know how to take this. He knew he was lying, and he knew that I knew it. He realized that I could have really embarrassed him if I had wanted to. I think that incident made us much closer buddies."

LEAVE IT TO JAMERSON

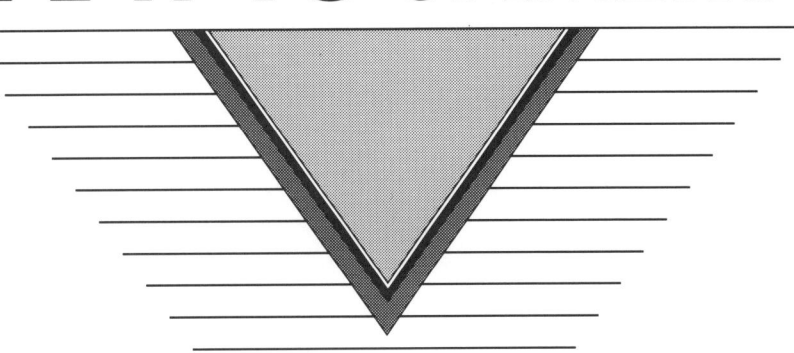

If you had stopped over for a visit at the Jamerson house during the mid-sixties and expected to find "Mr. Motown Bass," you would probably have left very disappointed. In place of "Igor—the King of Funk," you would have found a simple family man who was more a combination of Ward Cleaver and Julia Child than Ray Brown and Paul Chambers. (Well, maybe a funkified version of Ward Cleaver.) While I wouldn't go so far as to compare James' wife and his two eldest sons to June, Wally, and the Beaver, the Jamerson clan was enjoying a period of upper-middle class prosperity and happiness prior to the onset of James' drinking and career problems of the seventies and early eighties.

"James really spoiled the kids," reminisces Annie. "They each had $5.00 a week allowances and more toys than they knew what to do with. He'd take us out to fancy restaurants all the time, and every year, we'd go on vacations down south. We didn't want for anything. Whatever we asked for, we got." According to Robert White, James went out of his way to take care of his family because they were an important part of his emotional stability:

"Jamerson had tunnel vision. His entire world was his music and his family. He didn't have that many outside interersts. Anne Jamerson was a very strong woman and James knew she was always in his corner. I think his wife was a very important reason that he was still alive in the seventies. If not for her faith in God, and loving him in spite of everything he did, I don't think Jamerson could have made it. And his relationship with his children was also very special. He talked about them all the time. His kids, and kids in general always loved him because he was a child at heart. He was just a big kid himself."

The house that Jamerson purchased in 1964. This is where he lived during his glory period when he was cranking out masterpieces like "Bernadette," "I Was Made to Love Her," and "Ain't No Mountain High Enough."

By 1966, James' fourth and last child, Derek, was born. The family now consisted of James Jr., Joey, Dorene (who was nicknamed Penny), and baby Derek. The more the merrier for James, as he now had the chance to relive his childhood in a happier and more hospitable environment. However, it was difficult sometimes to figure out exactly who was the parent and who was the child in the Jamerson house. Annie recalls hearing the kids often going through one of the essential rituals of the American family experience—arguing over television rights. Af-

The Jamerson clan in 1967. From left to right: James Jr., Joey, James' Aunt Evalina MacKnight, Derek (seated), Penny, James, James' mother Elizabeth, and Annie.

ter all, difficult decisions like whether to watch *Roadrunner, Yogi Bear, Batman,* or *Godzilla Eats New York* shouldn't be taken lightly. But when Annie would go downstairs to check out what all the commotion was about, she would usually find that the center of the argument was James...Sr! (He usually cast his vote for *Yogi Bear*.)

Anyone as creative as James Jamerson was not going to sit down with his kids and play *Monopoly* or some other store bought game. He devised his own favorites, like his dragon imitation during which he chased the kids around the house in the morning, inflicting them with his bad breath (occasionally after a hard night of drinking and smoking). Another of his "greatest hits" was his habit of making the kids think that something was wrong with "old Dad" as he talked at length with his invisible dog. Penny fondly remembers her father playing his upright bass and dancing around with the kids in the living room, or picking them up and playing them as if they were a Fender Precision, while his mouth mimicked a walking bass line.

That's about as close as James wanted to get to his bass when he wasn't gigging or recording. He regarded his home as a refuge from the pressures of the studio and his busy schedule. Although his instruments were always laying around the house, playing music was a low priority when Jamerson was at home with his family. Other than occasionally coaching young James Jr. on the bass, or playing musical games with the kids, James rarely touched his instruments when he was away from the studio and the club scene. Practice was something he did on the job. According to James Jr., his father didn't even like Motown records to be played around the house:

"He'd come home from the studio and say, 'Turn that off. I have to play that stuff all day long and I don't want to have to listen to it when I come home.' Usually, he would just listen to Jazz around the house—mostly keyboard and sax players. When we'd come home after school and hear jazz playing on the stereo, we'd say, 'Dad's home.' I remember he used to play Oscar Peterson so much that it would make me sick."

And speaking of being made sick . . . James' family and friends were always subjected to his curious culinary habits. If you were a guest at the Jamerson house, you had to eat. James loved to cook, but as one of his friends told me, "He didn't cook normal stuff. He liked to cook all that gichee food like raccoon, rabbit, possum, and different kinds of gumbos with rice. He made all kinds of weird concoctions. Some of them tasted pretty good, particularly the crabs and seafood stuff he made, but they were all spicy. He loved that hot sauce."

James also had a habit of picking up several bags of Chinese food, chicken, or barbequed ribs after his recording sessions and club dates, and then waking up Annie and the kids at two or three o'clock in the morning for a late night food orgy. "Food was almost like a hobby for James whether it was eating it or cooking it," recalls Annie. "He used to get a real kick out of trying out his new recipes on his friends and the family. He was probably more sensitive about his cooking than he was about his bass playing. If you didn't like something that James made, he would really get hurt and upset."

If that was the Jamerson family's biggest problem, life would have been a breeze. Unfortunately, the real trials would begin a few years later in 1969.

DR. JAMERSON & MR. HYDE

> *"Men who produce works of genius are not those who live in the most delicate atmosphere, whose conversation is most brilliant or their culture broadest, but those who have had the power, ceasing in a moment to live only for themselves, to make use of their personality as of a mirror."*
>
> *Marcel Proust- Remembrance of Things Past: Within a Budding Grove (1913-1927)*

Marcel Proust must have been hanging out at the Chit Chat club, because he certainly sounds like he had James Jamerson's number. More than half a century ago, the great French novelist showed his understanding of the unique relationship between the personalities of gifted people and the art that they create. Just as the elegance and style of Duke Ellington comes across in some of his masterpieces like "Black and Tan Fantasy," and the torment and loneliness of Vincent Van Gogh almost jumps off the canvas in works like "The Night Cafe," Jamerson's life and character traits were also shadowed by his art. At times, he could be as complex as the bass lines from "Bernadette," or as simple and straightforward as the intro he created on "My Girl."

It was impossible to know James Jamerson and have a blasé take-it-or-leave-it opinion of him. Regardless of his ever changing moods, for better or for worse, James always made a strong impression on everyone he met. West Coast studio guitarist David T. Walker explains, "He was a different kind of person. When I first met him, it was around '65 or '66 at a Motown picnic on Belle Isle. All these people were partying and playing games, but he was off by himself fishing—he was a loner. A lot of the people who didn't understand him usually didn't take the time to get to know him...I think they really missed out."

"We knew where he was coming from and we loved him," adds Robert White, "but a lot of other people didn't want to be around him because of his unusual behavior. I don't know what they were afraid of because Jamerson never really harmed anybody but himself. He was really a nice person. First of all, he was a kind guy. He'd give you the shirt off his back. Instant gratification was the name of his game, but he was also a guy who would sit down and listen to your problems. If your car was broken down, he would pick you up and take you wherever you needed to go that day, because he had nothing better to do than play music or help someone."

In the early days, Motown stars were very familiar with James' generosity, whether it was a case of chauffeuring them to rehearsals and recording sessions, or bringing them home to his house to help drill their vocal harmonies. Temptations' "basso profundo," Melvin Franklin recalls, "Jamerson kind of took me under his wing because I was the bass singer, so we related on that level. He taught me always to make sure that I could hear one (scale degree one of the key) in my head and that way I'd never get lost in the harmony. I used to ask him things 'cause I always wanted to know, and I'd sit down for hours and hours and listen to his patterns and runs and how he did things. I admired him so much, it was hard for him not to like me."

However, Jamerson's musical tutorials weren't limited to just Motowners. As saxophonist Grover Washington Jr. observes, "He was very gracious and accessible when I met him. He was like a musical father. He would give a lot of the younger players direction whether they played bass or not, and it was always constructive criticism. It was never destructive. He would say, 'Well, why don't you play it this way because . . .' as opposed to just saying, 'Hey man, you're playing that wrong.' That has stuck with me in my career because it's helped me get closer to my band."

All this tends to make James sound like a choirboy, and at times he was, but there was also a darker side that was always lurking behind every liquor bottle. As Earl Van Dyke sadly points out, "When Benny was drunk, he would get playful, but when Jamerson would be drinking, he became overbearing and argumentative. I got mad at him once and said to him, 'Jamerson, why the hell do you drink so damn much?,' and he said, 'Cause' I like the taste of it.' I couldn't really say too much to him because I was a reformed drug addict myself."

Fighting and arguing weren't the only manifestations of James' inner turmoil. As territorial as he was when it came to other bassists showing up in the studio, it was nothing compared to his legendary jealousy for his wife. "When James was drinking, he would often start accusing me or other people of something," says Annie. "It was almost like that movie, *Raging Bull*, but I wasn't a flirt. I think James and I would have gone out on the town a lot more if he hadn't been so jealous. He didn't even like anyone looking at me.

"The funny thing was, he never thought he was a jealous person. We were on the road with the Miracles one night in 1963, and we were all sitting around the dressing room and somehow the subject of jealousy came up. Everyone was throwing out ideas and all of a sudden, James chimes in, 'Well, I'm glad I'm not a jealous type of person.' The second he said that, the whole room lit up and you heard five different people say at the exact same time, 'Oh, man . . .'"

But even though alcohol played a major role in Jamerson's behavior, there were other factors that had much deeper origins. The erratic and sometimes violent tendencies that he displayed probably owed just as much to the assortment of insecurities and fears that he carried throughout his life. For example, people who didn't take the time to get past his facade of aloofness never realized that he behaved that way to cover up his anxiety over his bad diction and general inability to express himself. However, if it was a one-on-one conversation with someone he felt comfortable with, he'd talk their head off.

The word "moderation" did not exist in James' vocabulary. Whether it was music, drinking, or jealousy, everything was carried to extremes. Even the practical jokes that he loved to play on some of his friends occasionally went a bit too far. His neighborhood drinking buddies may laugh about it today, but twenty years ago, they probably weren't too happy about being locked inside a neighborhood bar for an entire afternoon as a result of one of Jamerson's pranks. After downing a few beers with his friends at Jack and Joe's bar, James said his goodbyes and then coolly pulled his car up on the sidewalk against the building, preventing the doors to the only exit from swinging out. After admiring his handiwork, James walked home for dinner with the sweet music of his prisoners' curses ringing in his ears.

Jamerson could definitely be wild and reckless when the mood struck him, but in keeping with his unpredictable, multi-faceted personality, he was also a person of deep mystical and spiritual conviction. While this certainly helped to counterbalance his stormy disposition, it also had a lot to do with his approach in dealing with other musicians and artists. He always tried to play not only to the song in question, but also to the personality of the star that he was dealing with. James felt that he could just look at someone and tell what type of bass line they needed. Frank Wilson explains, "He talked about God a lot. Somehow, he always felt that he was in touch with The Divine and he could know what another person was thinking, in both musical situations and in everyday life. I think this faith in God kept him alive a lot longer and helped make some sense out of his life. Even with all his problems, James had a great sense of humor, and he really had a positive outlook on life. It was an incredible dichotomy."

From the first day James arrived in Detroit until his death almost thirty years later, contradictions like these would confound his family, friends, and co-workers, as they struggled to understand the conflict that was raging within his soul. Even today, they still remain in the dark. Rather than try to place order into something that was by nature chaotic, perhaps it would make more sense to let the random thoughts of some of James' friends complete his eclectic portrait.

Martha Jean "The Queen" Steinberg - Detroit radio personality and community activist:

"His eyes and that wide forehead were so impressive. He was a nice looking guy, but you could never tell what was going on inside. He was a very quiet, secret man. Everybody knew that he was difficult, sensitive, feelings easily hurt, wore his feelings on his sleeve, but he was basically a nice guy. The other guys loved him and went along with him. Earl and Robert and the rest of the Funk Brothers gave him a family base, and although he went against the grain sometimes, he trusted them and felt comfortable with them.

"He was more or less an introvert who was waiting for someone to appreciate him for his talent. Jamerson was always waiting for approval but was afraid to ask for it. He was always fearful of rejection, so in his head, he decided not even to get into a position to be rejected. He would just withdraw into his bass because he knew he didn't have to be insecure about that. He knew he was bad on his axe and he acted like he was. When it came to his music, he was very arrogant, but not in a conceited way. He didn't talk . . . he just did it. You see, he heard things in his mind that no one else could, but somewhere down the line in his life, he couldn't get it together. The problems he had, well . . . most people are weird when they're that talented."

Paul Riser - Motown arranger:

"Jamerson's music was always the most important thing to him, and because of that, he could be difficult sometimes during sessions. I had my times with him where we almost got into actual fistfights, but the next day or even later on that evening, he would be like nothing ever happened . . . like, 'Hey brother, how you doin'.' He wasn't the type of guy who held grudges. Outside of that bottle, he was basically a very happy-go-lucky and mild mannered type of person."

Robert White - Motown guitarist:

"Jamerson lived in a complete fantasy world. You never knew when he was telling the truth, and you never knew when he was feeling bad. No matter how bad things got, he always had something good to say. He was never down on himself. He got a lot of living into a very short lifespan. He knew he was walking a tightrope, and he was aware of the risk he was taking. I think the lifestyle that Jamerson led eventually just burned him out, but I envied the guy a lot because he had a lot more experiences than I ever did. He was out having experiences while I was asleep."

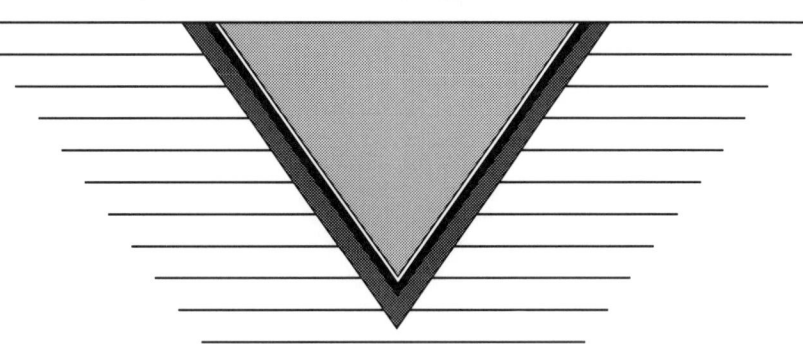
GROWING PAINS

> *"Change is the law of life. And those who look only to the past or the present are certain to miss the future."*
> -John F. Kennedy-
>
> *"Don't look back. Something might be gaining on you."*
> -Leroy "Satchell" Paige-

By 1971, the front office had just about had its fill of James Jamerson's continuing problems. According to the tally sheets in the accounting department, Motown was not getting very much of a return on their $52,000-a-year investment, and James was coming very close to being dropped from the roster of Hitsville's session players. Producer Frank Wilson recalls that if not for Berry Gordy interceding and refusing to allow this firing, James would have had to find a new record company or a new line of work.

What???? Just a couple of pages ago, he was doing so well! What could have possibly happened in a few short years to bring about such a dramatic change of attitudes and events? Even if James knew the answer to this question, the outcome would have probably been the same. His path, just like Motown's, had become too complicated to be controlled.

Like a deep-sea diver who ascends to the surface too quickly, Motown was going through a bad case of the bends. Even a master of the arts of creative visualization and positive mental attitude like Berry Gordy could never have envisioned in 1958 just how far his parents' $700 loan would take him. By the late sixties, Motown had become the largest black-owned company in the United States, with a yearly gross income in the tens of millions. Gordy's one house operation had expanded to six houses after he bought five more buildings on the same block. In fact, Motown acquired a lot of new toys. When they grew tired of the crosstown competition from Ed Wingate's Golden World studios, Motown bought him out. And when their operation outgrew the five newly acquired properties on West Grand Boulevard, they purchased a ten-story building downtown on Woodward Street and promptly moved in with their entire front office.

One of the first casualties of the company's meteoric rise was the intimate family concept that had been stressed from day one. In the harsh reality of recognition by everyone that Motown had become big business, drug and alcohol problems, financial disenchantment, and overblown egos began to rock the foundation of the company. The Temptations would be devastated by the departures of David Ruffin in '68, Eddie Kendricks in '71, and the tragic suicide of their baritone singer, Paul Williams in August of '73. Only Melvin Franklin and Otis Williams were left to carry on the tradition. The Supremes would follow a similar scenario with the exit of Florence Ballard in '67 and the flowering of Diana Ross' solo career in 1970. The Isely Brothers chose to pioneer their own record label and leave with all members intact, rather than follow the path of slow death that had befallen the Marvelettes, the Contours, Martha and the Vandellas, and some of the other acts that Motown had put on the back burner. Perhaps the biggest blow of all was the loss of Motown's most consistent hitmakers, the songwriting-production team of Holland-Dozier-Holland. In 1968, they too moved on, and eventually established their own record labels—Invictus and Hot Wax.

Growing Pains

While it may seem that the house that Berry built was collapsing, in actuality, the company was just going through a retooling period—a changing of the guard. The mass exodus of talent from Hitsville's roster was a testimonial to the resilience and depth of Gordy's creation. Lesser companies might have faltered. Instead, the final phase of Motown's glorious Detroit era got underway. Even though Stevie Wonder, the Miracles, Marvin Gaye, the Four Tops, and a revamped version of the Temptations would continue to be Motown's bread and butter, new acts were beginning to emerge to take the place of departed artists and fading stars. During the company's last five years in "the Motor City," Gladys Knight and the Pips, Edwin Starr, the Jackson Five, Bobby Taylor and the Vancouvers, the Originals, and the Undisputed Truth would all come to the forefront and make major contributions towards upholding the Hitsville tradition. Motown would survive all these new changes and head into the seventies with high hopes . . . but for one man, it just wasn't going to be as much fun.

1968 looked like it was going to be a good year for James. The new bass style that he had been perfecting throughout the sixties had now reached full maturity. His bass lines on hits like "I'm Gonna Make You Love Me," "For Once In My Life," and "Shoo-Be-Doo-Be-Doo-Da-Day" were causing producers and musicians to shake their heads in awe. James was exploring uncharted realms of funk with each new track that he played on, and it was becoming apparent to everyone at Motown that his creativity was almost limitless.

Progressing right along with Jamerson's musical explorations was his bank account, which was also expanding into new territory—the land of financial security. James had asked Motown for a salary of $1000 a week and the company agreed to his demands. The $52,000-a-year that the company was now paying him did not include bonuses, club work, and occasional moonlighting sessions with other record companies. By 1968 standards, he was becoming a wealthy man. James had worked hard to become the king of the R&B bass world, but the peace and serenity of his domain would be short-lived. The relative security and contentment that he had finally achieved was about to be challenged from many different directions. Perhaps one of the first and most painful of these hardships was the death of the man whose musical groove James had depended on for almost a decade.

Whenever Motown recording stars became too big for their britches, Benny Benjamin could always be counted upon to put them back in their place by saying, "I've been down in this studio from the very beginning, and I've seen them come and go, but I'm still here." Unfortunately by the late sixties, Benny could no longer say that. He had been slipping for several years as a result of a car accident that hurled him through a windshield and left his skin full of inoperable glass fragments. However, it was his long standing heroin addiction that did most of the damage and finally ended his life. At the 1967 recording session for Gladys Knight and the Pips' "I Heard it Through the Grapevine," Benny was so weak that he could only play light fills on the cymbals. His legendary sense of time had deteriorated to the point where his protege´, Uriel Jones, had to play the main groove. Benny would hold on for almost two more years, but his recording schedule was drastically reduced. When he passed away in 1969, all of Motown was grief-stricken. James Jamerson would later tell Nelson George in an interview, "Oh man, he was my favorite. When he died, I couldn't eat for two weeks, it hurt me so bad."[5]

For the rest of the Funk Brothers, life in "the Snakepit" went on. The acts *were* coming and going, but James, Earl, Robert, and the rest of the gang were still there, continuing to be the heartbeat and the continuity that ran through "the Motown Sound." There were some modifications, however. Some new kids arrived on the block—the most significant being guitarists Dennis Coffey and Melvin (Wah Wah Watson) Ragin, who arrived in 1968 to expand the colors of Motown's guitar palette. Bassist Bob Babbitt was also added the same year to help cover the rapidly expanding recording schedule. In the void left following Benny's death, Uriel Jones and Pistol Allen would begin to assume more important roles, and drummer Andrew Smith, who came into Hitsville as a 17-year-old prodigy in 1967, would become an increasingly

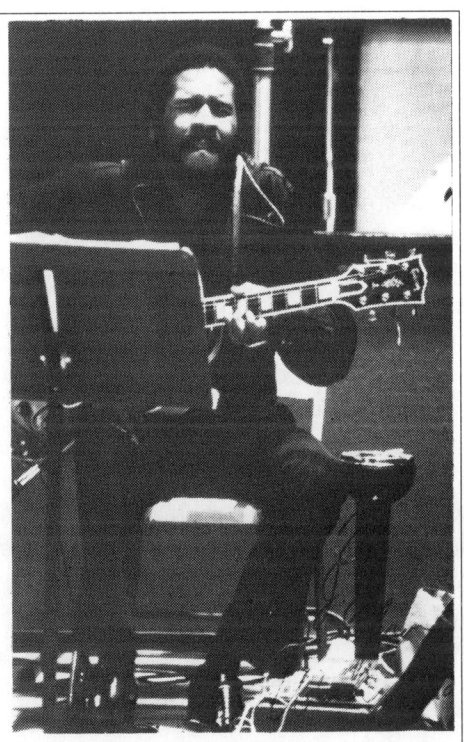

Dennis Coffey | Wah Wah Watson

familiar face during the sessions.

These personnel changes were necessitated in part by Motown's busy recording schedule following the acquisition of Golden World. The Snakepit was now called Studio "A" and Golden World was dubbed Studio "B." Even though Hitsville's original studio still reigned supreme when it came to R&B rhythm section tracks, the new studio was kept very busy with string and horn overdubs. It was also a big part of Motown's budding Rare Earth label which was intended to introduce Motown into the white FM underground market. Acts like Rare Earth and R. Dean Taylor ("Indiana Wants Me") also needed bass tracks laid down, and since Jamerson couldn't be in two places at the same time, new bass players were recruited. Even though he realized they were necessary, all these new bassists moving in on his turf made the territorial Jamerson very uneasy. However, he eventually made peace with the new order of things and even became good friends with Babbitt, Michael Henderson, and a few of the other Motown "rookies."

Along with all the personnel changes, Motown's arranging staff implemented a new level of musical sophistication that was drastically different from all the freedom that Jamerson and the rest of the Funk Brothers enjoyed in the mid-sixties. Arranger Dave Van de Pitte recalls:

"There were 25 to 30 producers and 75-100 songwriters in the company at that time, and they'd put together a piano demo and then it was on the arrangers. We were in on the projects from the ground floor. It wasn't just a matter of sweetening a basic rhythhm track anymore. You had to transcribe the demo tapes and then start writing. The rhythm charts changed around this time too—they became very specific. They were composite two or three line charts that were basically glorified piano parts, with the left hand written in for the bass player. In the middle somewhere, we would have drum parts written in with any cues and a general drum beat, and in the right hand were any piano voicings and guitar chords. Some of them were quite elaborate. We used composites because everybody knew what everyone else was doing all of the time and it was very simple to make corrections out on the floor."

These expanded production policies may have been great for the arrangers, songwriters, and producers, but the thrill was no longer there in the same way for the musicians. For years, producers had turned to the Funk

Brothers to help them come up with ideas—however, this was no longer the case. By the late sixties, the spotlight had shifted to the people with the pencils, and the musicians were now just basically "reading the paper." For someone like Jamerson who relished his center-stage role, this was a difficult demotion to take.

Another new policy that he had trouble adapting to was Motown's practice of cutting tracks on the West Coast (and occasionally in New York) with other bassists. Now James felt that his job was being threatened not only from Detroit, but from cities thousands of miles away. Dennis Coffey explains, "Since about 1966 or so, Motown was trying to establish a beachhead in California, but I think that they were so afraid of doing something without him, that they were constantly flying tracks back here and overdubbing the bass. 'Reflections' was one of those tunes that he had to overdub. Jamerson just couldn't understand why the hell they didn't use him in the first place."

With all of these insecurities constantly plaguing him, James' drinking entered a new phase. He was no longer a social drinker or "the hard partier" that Smokey Robinson described earlier. Alcohol was now becoming a problem both to James and to Motown, as his performance and demeanor in the studio began to change. Robert White explains, "That whole pressure thing at Motown did put a lot of stress on the guy because as Motown got more sophisticated, so did the demands on the musicians. It was hard for *all* the musicians to adjust to the change that Motown was going through, but Jamerson in particular had a rough time."

Alcohol was not the direct cause of his musical fall-off, but the resulting moodiness that his drinking created brought about the same results. As Wah Wah Watson explains, "I've seen him when he was 'feeling good,' but when the music started, it was all over. He played! But sometimes, when something went wrong, or a producer or someone pissed him off, he wouldn't play. I mean, he would play but . . . it wouldn't be the same James."

The Funk Brothers knew how to deal with Jamerson when he became entrenched in one of his moods. Earl Van Dyke, who was somewhat of an authoritative father-figure to James was usually able to straighten him out with a few well chosen stern words, but sometimes it took a more creative approach as Wah Wah relates:

"Jamerson had these messed up feet, y'know? He used to wear these high-top boots, and he had all these corns that used to stick out the side of his shoes. It looked like he had marbles in there with his feet. He used to take them boots off when his corns hurt and those toes would be dangling in the air. I used to drive him crazy chasing him around the room fakin' like I was gonna' step on his corns. If you ever wanted to get his attention, all you had to do was just stand by him and stomp near his feet. Sometimes, you had to do stuff like that to cool him out. We had a lot of fun with him. It was really funny. I mean . . . even today, if you go up to one of the other Funk Brothers and they're acting real serious, just say, 'Hey man, how bad was Jamerson's feet?' and you watch, they'll open right up."

If all else failed and there was a serious need to lighten things up, there was always "the Dozens." Translated into plain English, this refers to the fine art of cutting up someone's mother. The Funk Brothers had been doing it for years, but with the addition of Wah Wah, "the Dozens" reached heights that they had only dreamed of in the past. Robert White reminisces:

"The champions of 'the Dozens' was Wawa and Eddie 'Bongo' Brown was second. The guys would come up with the funniest stories about another guy's mother. Eddie Bongo was the most original and Wawa was probably the most vicious. Jamerson was the stupidest because he really didn't believe in it at all. He was very awkward talking about another person's mother because he was like myself, very respectful of his mother. He also was not very articulate when speaking. His diction was bad, but he tried to keep up and be one of the guys. But the more he tried, the worse he sounded. He was kind of funny—like a guy who tells a joke and gets it all backwards. They would wipe up the floor with him. They would just kill him, but he wanted to be part of the action."

James wasn't always the fall guy, however. He could dish it out with the best of them, as drummer Andrew

Smith found out during one afternoon session at Hitsville:

"I had just started working at Motown and I was in awe of everybody because I was just a kid out of high school. Well, one day Jamerson said that he wanted to take me out for lunch in between the morning and afternoon sessions, but all the rest of the guys started screaming, 'No, don't do it— you'll be sorry.' I thought they were crazy because here was this legend asking me to lunch. I felt honored. Anyway, when lunchtime came around, we took off in James' car and he drove a few blocks away to a grocery store. A few minutes later, he comes walking out with a bottle of Metaxa (Greek brandy) and a pound of grapes and starts eating them. I figured that he was just doing some shopping on the way to the restaurant, and I said to him, 'Where are we going for lunch?' He looked at me and said, 'This is lunch.' Well, when I got back to the studio, I was messed up, and everybody was laughing at me saying, 'I told you not to go with him.' Jamerson was laughing too."

Unfortunately, most of the anecdotes surrounding Jamerson's drinking problems during Motown's last years in Detroit didn't make people laugh. In hopes of straightening him out, Motown tried a little psychology by appointing him as the director of the workshops that were taking place upstairs at Golden World. The workshops were rehearsal sessions used to develop new grooves in a less pressurized atmosphere than the recording studio. Motown also took advantage of these brainstorming sessions by using them to weed out some people in the production staff. The recording process had become very wasteful, so this was a good opportunity for the front office to find out which producers were just marking time. While these sessions didn't help very much in solving Jamerson's problems, they did help Motown to find out who would be the man to pick up the torch relinquished by the departed Holland-Dozier-Holland production team.

Norman Whitfield wasn't a newcomer by any means. He had sat on the steps of the Snakepit as an observer for almost two years, absorbing every bit of studio savvy that he could before working up the courage to produce the 1964 Marvelettes hit, "Too Many Fish in the Sea." Starting in '66 with "Ain't Too Proud to Beg," Norman would go on a tear with the Temptations that would last for the next five years, but it wasn't until the evolution of his Sly Stone inspired funk epics like "Cloud Nine," "Smiling Faces Sometimes," and "Papa Was A Rolling Stone," that Motown would consider his talents valuable enough to sign him to a multi-million dollar production contract. Utilizing the new guitar concepts brought in by Dennis Coffey and Wah Wah Watson, Whitfield was taking the Motown Sound in a radically different direction. As the Supremes' pop style of the mid-sixties began to sink into the West, Whitfield's stock began to rise, and Motown began to view him as the man who would lead them into the seventies.

Motown's quest for fresh sounds and new directions was reflected by the innovation of their double drummer and double bass sessions. The double drummer sessions allowed complex beats to be divided up between

James playing at Stevie Wonder's wedding. The drummer is Hamilton Bohannon.

two players, allowing them to concentrate on feel rather than being burdened by technical problems. During Motown's final years in Detroit, these sessions became increasingly common. The double bass sessions however, were not always as successful as Robert White testifies:

"They would take a low bass line that was just doing the fundamental like a bass tuba part, and another guy would be an octave up doing the actual playing. The lower part was written out and the upper part, which was usually Jamerson, was just fakin' it reading the chords. Sometimes they would dump the low part after they were finished."

Bob Babbit has a more humorous and less scientific memory of the approach being used: "The producers would usually say something to James like, 'You play everything that he doesn't play,' and then they'd point to me and say, 'You play everything that Jamerson doesn't play.'" Whatever the procedure was, most of the Funk Brothers agree that the majority of these sessions wound up in the trash. "We didn't particularly care for the sound," says Joe Messina. "It was very muddy. Most of those sessions were experimental."

One experiment that turned out a bit more successfully was the grooming of a family act from Gary, Indiana that was fronted by a dynamic ten-year-old lead singer named Michael. Whether Jamerson played on the Jackson Five's first two hits, "I Want You Back" and "ABC," is a very cloudy area. The bass lines and tone are reminiscent of Jamerson, but that doesn't necessarily prove anything. By the late 60's, most of Motown's bassists and arrangers tried to emulate James' style when they performed or wrote out bass lines.

Asking some of the musicians and producers only adds to the confusion. Freddie Perren, who was a member of "the Corporation" production team, insists that both songs were cut on the West Coast with Wilton Felder on bass. David T. Walker, who played guitar on all the early Jackson Five material, remembers the tracks as being played by either Wilton or Ron Brown. Ron Brown maintains that Jamerson flew out to the West Coast in '69 to cut the tracks. Dennis Coffey says that he played on "ABC" and "I Want You Back" in Detroit with Jamerson. Bob Babbitt claims that he was the bassist on those sessions, and still other Motown musicians recall the tracks being flown back to Detroit from L.A. so that Jamerson could overdub his bass.

One fact that is certain is that the rise of the Jackson Five signaled an alarming trend in Motown's production philosophy concerning the bass; they became aware that they could crank out hits *without* James Jamerson. Even if James did play on the two songs in question, most of the Jackson Five material was recorded on the West Coast by other bassists. In addition, some other Motown stars and producers who had kept James working for years, were also beginning to cut with other bassists. The Temptations cut with Bob Babbitt when they recorded their 1970 smash, "Ball of Confusion," and Stevie Wonder did not use James when he laid down tracks for "Sign, Sealed, Delivered" (the honor was claimed by both Bob Babbitt and Michael Henderson). Within a few years, Stevie wouldn't use a bass player at all. Synthesizers became the dominant sound throughout his 1972 *"Music of My Mind- Talking Book"* period.

However, the biggest setback for James at this time came as a result of falling out with producer Norman Whitfield. Jamerson never particularly liked anyone telling him how to play his instrument, so he and Norman were destined from the start for a big time collision; Norman was just as headstrong as Jamerson, and he loved to tell everyone how to play. But Bob Babbitt explains that there was much more to this situation than just conflicting musical egos: "At first, Norman started using me because Jamerson had broken his hand and was out of commission for a few weeks, but there was also another reason. Norman came up to me one day and said, 'Bob, I want to use you on some dates because lately, Jamerson has been showing up at the studio with his eyes in the back of his head.'" In any case, Norman eventually began to use James again, and there was still plenty of work for him at Motown—but the writing was on the wall and he knew it.

Throughout the sixties, James' family had always been his emotional security blanket when things were going wrong. He was always able to leave his anxieties and career problems in the studio, but as the seventies approached, the rage that was building within him began to surface at home. Annie explains, "The kids and I had to walk on eggshells to accommodate his moods. Sometimes, he would get very belligerent and argumentative, but I hung in there because the next day when he was sober, he could be the sweetest person in the world. He just didn't know what he wanted. I remember a few times he just started crying and telling me, 'Baby, I don't know what to do. I'm confused.' But then he would go in the bathroom and wash his face and he'd come out screaming and angry again."

In 1970, Annie and James had been contemplating moving into a new house in the affluent Sherwood Forest section of Detroit. "It was our dreamhouse," Annie recalls wistfully. "It had five bedrooms, a sunken Japanese garden, and sliding doors and big picture windows all over the place, but I told James that if he didn't straighten up his act, there was no sense in our buying it. I wasn't going to put up with all the craziness any more. He was really putting us all through some changes, and the kids, who were getting into their teens by then, needed a better role model. He said, 'I know baby. I'll try to get myself together,' and he did for a little while. But once we moved into the new house in 1971, he got much worse. I remember Smokey came over for the housewarming party, and he asked me if I was happy. I told him, 'No, I guess there's more to life than just a big house and money.'"

In the studio, Jamerson was acting out a comparable scenario. As more and more procedural changes were implemented by Motown, James became increasingly disenchanted, and his behavior reflected it. Promotion man Weldon McDougal points out, "It got to the point where the company would not rely on Jamerson at all because if you booked him on a gig or a recording session, you had to take the chance that he might not come. It was hard to figure out how to handle him because on one hand, he was trouble, but on the other hand, he was the world's greatest bass player. Everyone wanted to use him but you didn't know when he was going to be stable. I remember one time, he flipped out in the studio and destroyed some acoustic paneling. He was really causing some problems."

So now you know why Motown was ready to can Jamerson. Berry Gordy's intervention may have been an unexpected development to some of the people in the front office, but it didn't surprise Frank Wilson at all. "One thing about Berry—he always appreciated loyalty,

The "dream house." Annie with Derek and Penny in 1971 outside of their new five bedroom home in the Sherwood Forest section of Detroit.

and as big a problem as James had become at that time, he had been with Motown almost from the beginning." But aside from Berry's sense of loyalty being the possible motivation for saving Jamerson's job, he may have also felt that James still had a lot of music left in him. During the early part of the same year, Jamerson had performed brilliantly on Marvin Gaye's *What's Going On* album.

Marvin, coming out of a two year slump brought on by marital problems, drugs, and depression over the death of his friend and singing partner, Tammi Terrell, would create the masterpiece of his career in this inspired work. *What's Going On* would lay waste to all of the production concepts that Motown had developed over the previous decade. The songs were too long, too topical, and too unfocused for Motown's pop tastes. They weren't even sure at first if they were going to release it at all, but once it hit the market, *What's Going On* wound up breaking all of Motown's sales records with over 8,000,000 copies sold in the U.S. alone.

There was no way that Marvin was going to record *What's Going On* without James. Marvin had always been one of Jamerson's biggest fans within the company, and the two of them had a special chemistry whenever they worked together that seemed to bring out their best efforts. Some of Jamerson's finest work is found on Marvin Gaye tracks like "Ain't That Peculiar," "Chained," and "Ain't Nothing Like the Real Thing." James must have really been impressed by the finished track of "What's Going On," because Annie recalls him coming home after the session and referring to it as a masterpiece. "That was pretty rare for James," says Annie, "because he hardly ever talked about what happened at work once he came home."

Still, according to Dave Van dePitte, who arranged the entire *What's Going On* album, James had to be prodded to contribute anything more than just reading the charts:

"After the late sixties, Jamerson had a certain attitude that he wasn't going to give you any more than he had to. If you wrote something down that he had played before or you could find a lick, he would take that lick and he would elaborate on it. He could remember bass lines that he had played 10 years ago for the company. Producers would say to him, 'James you remember the bass line you played on such and such a tune?,' and he'd say, 'Oh yeah,' and he'd play it. Then they'd say, 'Well that's the kind of feel I want on this tune. Do you think you could do that and spice it up a little bit?' Sometimes it could get really out of hand and sound like a bass concerto. He would come out with some of the most outlandish things that you ever heard in your life. I mean, they were great but they had no place in what you were doing. I think he just did that for effect to show everybody that he hadn't lost any technique. On "What's Going On" though, he just read the part down like I wrote it. He loved it because I had written Jamerson licks for James Jamerson."

"Mr. Slick" and Annie out for a night on the town.

James would tell his friends in later years that he had recorded one of the tracks on the *What's Going On* album lying flat on his back. As the story goes, Marvin had unexpectedly stopped by a club where James was playing and asked him to drop by the studio after the last set. James had been on a week-long drinking binge and had been planning on going directly home after the job for a much-needed night of sleep. When he arrived at the studio, he was so drunk and tired that he could barely sit upright in the chair, so he laid down on the floor and played the song. (This story supports the contention of most of the Motown musicians, producers, and arrangers that alcohol usually had very little effect on his musical performance in the studio. Dave Van dePitte points out, "Jamerson always kept a bottle of Metaxa in his bass case. He could really put that stuff away, and then sit down and still be able to play. His tolerance was incredible. It took a hell of a lot to get him smashed.")

While *What's Going On* was expanding the boundaries of Rhythm and Blues, it was also breaking ground in a completely different direction—it was the first successful album in Motown's history that listed musicians' credits. (There was actually an obscure Valerie Simpson album that listed credits before *What's Going On*, but since it sold very little, the recognition factor and its impact upon the musicians is generally overlooked.) Money had never really been Jamerson's gripe. Motown usually gave him what he asked for on the financial end, but recognition was another matter entirely. The growing realization that he was having a massive impact on pop music, and still no one knew who he was, began to eat away at him. It has long been rumored that Motown tried to hide its studio players in secrecy to protect the company sound, but according to Smokey Robinson, the reason behind the lack of album credits was far less complex. "No other record companies at the time were crediting musicians so why were we supposed to?," says Smokey.

Smokey's explanation is backed up by the fifties and sixties records put out by Chess, VeeJay, Brunswick, Cameo Parkway, and all the other major R&B labels. They also omitted musicians' credits in their liner notes. The rare exception to this situation was the celebrity status enjoyed by "the Memphis Sound's" studio wizards, Booker T. and the MG's. They were the only session players of the sixties who actually became stars. But aside from their own releases, they too were passed over when credits were listed on albums by Sam and Dave, Otis Redding, and the rest of the acts in the Stax-Volt stable. It wasn't until 1968 and 1969 that Atlantic, Stax, Volt, and Atco changed their policy and began acknowledging back-up musicians. While Motown may not have been the first of the R&B labels to begin crediting studio musicians, they weren't exactly the last either.

This situation was typical of many of Jamerson's problems in the late sixties and early seventies. The times he lived in probably had more to do with his unhappy predicament than any front office "bad guys." In the eighties, if you so much as sneeze on a record, it's commonplace to receive full album credit, but back in the sixties, the idea was not yet implanted into the consciousness of the recording industry. The role of the studio musician as a star in their own right is a seventies' and eighties' concept. Similarly, drug and alcohol problems today are called substance abuse, and companies (sports teams in particular) generally try to help their employees by placing them in rehabilitation programs. In the sixties though, it was a different story. You were considered a drunk or a junkie, and people just tended to write off the offender.

But Motown didn't exactly write off James. While some may argue that it was too little, too late, they did make some overtures in the early seventies to honor him and recognize his contributions. For example, on the Four Tops' *Nature Planned It* album, Jamerson's credit reads: "Bass (Personified).........James Jamerson." Drummer Andrew Smith also recalls talk of either a solo record or a book featuring Jamerson's bass playing. "I don't know what became of those projects," says Andrew. "I have a feeling that James must have done something to turn off the front office...like playing outside recording sessions, or something like that, because after a while, we just didn't hear about it anymore." Another project that became lost in the shuffle was the recording of a James Jamerson-Dennis Coffey composition entitled "Fever in the

Funk House." Some veterans of Hitsville's early seventies studio lineup claim that the A&R department allowed Jamerson to cut this track just to placate him, but never really had any intentions of releasing it. However, as one musician observes, "When was Motown ever against making money? If the track was strong enough, it would have been released."

Nevertheless, the A&R department often showed James preferential treatment in the early seventies. Bending one of their longstanding rules, they allowed him to record some outside sessions during this period. (Most of them were with a variety of gospel acts, and there was also what should have been an historic early seventies session with British guitar legend, Jeff Beck. Unfortunately, nothing ever came of those tracks.) In addition, at a time when Motown was making drastic budget cuts and changing the salary and contract structures regarding most of it's musicians, Jamerson's financial and contractual situation remained unchanged—even though he was no longer as productive as he used to be.

Al McKay of Earth, Wind, and Fire recalls that during Motown's last year in Detroit, Jamerson was trying to compensate for the cutbacks in his Hitsville recording schedule by moonlighting as Pearl Bailey's bassist. "Around '71 and '72, I was the music director for the Sylvers who were opening up Pearl Bailey's shows at a place called Pine Knob in Detroit. James was playing with her at the time. Once I met him and found out who he actually was, I was there every night being gassed to death just watching him. He was such a great bass player. I guess his studio work had slowed down at the time."

It wouldn't be too long before everyone's studio work in Detroit would slow down. The fact that Motown's West Coast activities were constantly expanding did not escape the attention of the Funk Brothers and all the rest of Hitsville's employees. By 1972, the rumors that had been circulating around the company for over a year had now come to pass: Motown was definitely moving to Los Angeles. The Detroit studio operation was supposed to continue . . . at least for a while. Nevertheless, the musicians knew that they had better start looking around for another source of work.

It wasn't just the company that had changed. R&B, and Pop music in general, was undergoing a dramatic revolution, and the front office at Motown decided that the new groove they wanted to pursue was no longer going to be found in Detroit with home-grown musicians. "When Motown moved, that broke up a really precious family," notes Robert White with a trace of sadness in his voice. "The only member of the Funk Brothers that they took with them was Jamerson, and the rest of us felt a little deserted. But . . . things move on y'know? Anyway, we all felt good for James and wished him well. He'd earned the right to be where he was."

THE FALL OF THE KING

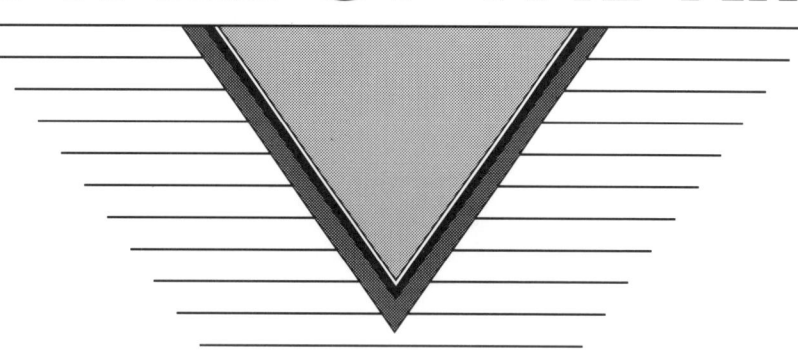

On a late summer night in 1973, several weeks before his departure to Los Angeles, James Jamerson picked up Joe Weaver and Chili Ruth and took them for a late night cruise in his shiny new Fleetwood. As they drove over the concrete bridge that connects Detroit to Belle Isle, his two closest friends could tell that he was agitated about something. In the next few hours, James would pour out all of his anxieties and fears over his impending move to Los Angeles. Somehow, he sensed that he would never return from this trip.

Like Robert White, a lot of Motown's Detroit crew were under the impression that the company had asked Jamerson to move out to Los Angeles to work for them. There actually had been talks between him and the A&R department but nothing ever came of these meetings. The move was really James' idea as a result of a West Coast vacation during which he had checked out the recording scene. He realized that he would no longer be "Igor," or "Funk," or "the Hook," because after all, this was a new territory where he would have to prove himself all over again. He would just be plain old James (or Jamie as he was called on the West Coast), but he decided to give it his best shot. It's not exactly like he wasn't welcome, however.

Even though Motown's West Coast operation had a new roster of studio musicians like Wilton Felder, Ron Brown, David T. Walker, Joe Sample, Ed Greene, and James Gadson, the A&R department was nevertheless ecstatic about Jamerson's move and instantly put him to work. Besides recording with Motown's established stars from the Detroit period, James was now cutting with Willie Hutch, G.C. Cameron, Yvonne Fair, and some of the other new acts that had been signed to the label.

In addition, James was now free to record or tour with any artist of his choice because Motown did not renew his contract. Although it was difficult for him to adjust to the idea that he was now just a freelance musician working with the company, as opposed to being the guy that everything revolved around, the advantages of his new status soon became obvious. In 1974, a combination of Motown and outside work kept James as busy as he had ever been. Tours with Marvin Gaye, Joan Baez, and Maria Muldaur, plus a full schedule of recording sessions for jingles, movie scores, TV themes like "S.W.A.T.," and some choice record dates with new acts like the Hues Corporation ("Rock the Boat") and Al Wilson ("Show and Tell") quickly sent out a strong message to the L.A. recording industry that James Jamerson was in town.

Producer Freddie Perren remembers James as being in top form when he first came out:

"He was very reserved on our sessions because it wasn't the Detroit click, but he was still playing great. I used Jamerson on a demo for a Temptations tune in early '74, along with Wah Wah Watson on guitar and James Gadson on drums. I wrote the parts out but I told Jamerson, 'Why don't you just go on and do your thing,' and he just laid the thing out so beautifully that there was no way in the world that I could have sat down at a desk and improved upon it. The bass line was what made Berry Gordy accept the tune."

The Fall of the King

The same year, arranger Gene Page (who conducted the '74 Marvin Gaye tour) jokingly tried to test Jamerson to see if he had lost anything, so he bet him $100 that he couldn't remember every note that he had played on "What's Going On." Gene should have stuck to arranging and conducting because this wager cost him a "C" note.

With his career once again on the rise and an entirely new and much larger market than Detroit awaiting him, things looked like they just might work out for James. He should have been very happy...but he wasn't. David T. Walker, who befriended Jamerson upon his 1973 arrival in Los Angeles recalls, "I showed him around when he first got out here. He was living in a motel at Sunset and Highland. He seemed okay, but I think he was a little lonely. I think he really missed his family. He didn't have a lot of friends outside of the studio. James more or less kept to himself, but he would call me and we would talk on the phone. I'd go over there and have some gumbo, or he'd invite me over to have some rabbit with him."

Unfortunately, rabbit wasn't the only strange thing James ate that year. With too many hours to spend alone, away from the moral support of his wife and kids, James quickly got into trouble. In the late fall of '73, James wound up being hospitalized for a bad reaction to a hallucinogenic drug. Paul Riser and a few of James' other friends insist that someone had spiked his drink at a party and James was unaware of it. There is probably some validity to this story because hallucinogenics were not usually a part of Jamerson's substance abuse arsenal. Nevertheless, this first brush with mortality put the fear of God in him, and he began to make a major effort towards putting his life in order.

James' spirits picked up a bit in the beginning of '74 when he bought a house in East Los Angeles and moved his family out. Besides the happiness that resulted from being reunited with Annie and the kids, James was very excited about the progress of his son's bass playing abilities. Apparently, so was the Los Angeles recording community because within a few short years, the sessions began rolling in for James Jr. as well. Hope and dreams were running high in the Jamerson house during this period, as plans were made for a "Jamerson & Son" conquest of the West Coast recording industry.

1975 started off with a major milestone in James' career—his very first (and only) gold record. Freddie Perren had hired him to play on the Sylver's recording of "Boogie Fever," and the track eventually reached the top ten. Even though the bass line on this tune is much more structured than the Jamerson improvisational style that everyone is accustomed to, James did a creditable job. He had obviously played on hundreds of gold and platinum recordings before "Boogie Fever," but this was the first one that was awarded to him. It may just have been a 45, but James Jr.

James on the road in the mid-seventies with a starry-eyed Maria Muldaur and her guitarist, Amos Garrett.

recalls that his Dad was smiling for weeks.

It would have been nice if this mood could have lasted a bit longer, but Jamerson was uncomfortable when things were going too smoothly. He usually felt more at home in the midst of some type of adversity. A few months later, the hopes and dreams of 1974 and the auspicious start of 1975 came crashing down when alcohol and attitude problems once again began to surface. James was sent home from Europe in the middle of a Diana Ross tour. Drinking wasn't the cause of this dismissal, but shortly after returning home, alcohol quickly became the source of a new wave of all too familiar career and personal setbacks. Frank Wilson recalls, "We'd try to talk to different people out here to get him booked on sessions, and then maybe he'd show, or he'd be late, or he would kind of space out on the session; and this made it more and more difficult for people to hire him."

Ben Barrett, who did most of the contracting for Motown and several other record companies in Los Angeles, was one of the people who eventually decided not to use Jamerson any more. "Producers began to complain about losing a recording session if he didn't show up," says Barrett. "We had talks. He was respectful, but he would be trying to hide his problems, saying that he didn't feel well or he had a cold, his car broke down, or he went to the wrong studio."

In Jamerson's defense, much of the behavior that was attributed to alcohol was actually a side effect of medication prescribed for him to help combat his substance abuse problems. The drugs may have eased his withdraw from alcohol, but they also dulled his senses and made his hands shake. James found himself in a situation where he was more or less chasing his tail. When he fouled up on a few sessions because of the effects of the medication, people would stop calling him for dates. When this would occur, James would get depressed and begin drinking again, which would perpetuate the cycle.

If it wasn't for the tragic results of the medication, some of the side effects it produced could be considered comical. James had begun hearing voices, and could

The gold record presented to James for his performance on the Sylver's hit, "Boogie Fever." The printing on the plaque that reads, "Presented to James Jamerson Jr." is confusing, because Motown bassist, James Jamerson was actually James Jr. The James Jr. who plays on the tape that accompanies this book is actually James Jamerson III.

occasionally be found talking to himself or some unknown being in the same room. One studio musician (who didn't want to be identified) recalled Jamerson talking to his hands one afternoon in the middle of a recording session. "All of a sudden, he looked at me real serious

The location may have changed but everything else remains the same.
This photo shows Jamerson hard at work during a West Coast
session with his 1962 P-bass, an Ampeg B-15, and most likely,
a very old, dead set of strings.

Both this shot and the one on the previous page were probably taken during the early part of Jamerson's California period. At this point in his life, his career and health were still in fairly good shape.

and says, 'My hands don't play on Tuesday.'" Frank Wilson's experience with James' "ghostly voices" was a bit more harrowing. Annie had asked him to help convince James to go back into the hospital for a prolonged cure, so Frank came over to the house and suggested that he and James take a car ride to talk. Jamerson was at the wheel when he suddenly stopped dead in the middle of the Los Angeles Freeway and told Frank that, "God had told him to stop."

James didn't exactly just roll over and die. For the entire ten years that he lived in Los Angeles, he battled his problems, and occasionally won for several months at a time. Right in the midst of one of his late seventies crises, James straightened himself out and played on a highly successful Aretha Franklin tour. Martha Jean Steinberg ran into him at a West Coast music convention during this period and could see that he was trying his best to pull his life together:

"He looked great and he said he hadn't been drinking for quite a while. He also told me that he turned to God and he was very involved with his church. It was almost as if he were a little kid saying, 'Mom, I know I've been bad, but look at me now. I'm good!' I only wish he could have stayed that way."

James didn't just drop from the music scene overnight like so many one-hit pop bands. His decline was slow and agonizing. David T. Walker maintains that even in the late 70's, there was still a lot of music left in him:

"In L.A., negative stories circulate very quickly. People began to be afraid to use him—which was unfortunate—because if they got him on a session, some magic was very possible. In his last few years because of some of the things he was doing, it was easy just to cancel on him and not want to be around him like some people did. I put the kind of time in with him that I did because he was such a beautiful person and such a great, creative artist. Sometimes his playing had gone downhill, but then at other times, there he was just knocking you out. I don't know how he did that.

"There were a few dates though where James was asked to leave. I used to sometimes pick him up before a record date so that he couldn't get anything to drink, and I would make sure that there was no liquor store on the way. But you couldn't watch him every minute. The last session I did with him, I had to help him through the door. It may have looked like alcohol was killing him, but he was really dying of heartbreak. He had done all this work and yet nobody would return his calls . . . and it wasn't just Motown."

Further aggravating Jamerson's condition was a deep depression over the fact that he could no longer support his family in the manner to which they were accustomed. Annie somberly remembers, "One day, I was in the kitchen cleaning the sink and James walked over to me with tears in his eyes and he pushed my hand off the sponge. It really hurt him that we couldn't afford to hire people to do that kind of work anymore. I didn't really mind that much, but he did."

Alcohol and emotional problems weren't the only cause of James' declining career. Most producers and studio musicians were aware of the possible assortment of difficulties that might arise when working with James, but his musicality had never been one of them. As one studio drummer recalls, "If he showed up, you could count on his bass playing like the Rock of Gibraltar." But as the mid-seventies approached, the rock started to show signs of cracking. Many of the problems resulted from Jamerson's inability to adjust to the differences between the Detroit and West Coast studio scenes. "In L.A., it was a 'just read the chart kind of thing,'" explains Dennis Coffey. "I would imagine that people there pushed him the wrong way initially by trying to make him fit into a certain mold. That was tough on him, because he was used to a lot more freedom."

Hank Cosby felt that the philosophical differences between the two cities' respective recording industries weren't the only obstacles facing his old friend. "In L.A., James was out of his element," says Hank. "He had been playing with the same group for 15 years. When Motown left, Jamerson was lost. He couldn't always lock in with the West Coast feel. The drummers and piano players were all playing different types of grooves than he was used to hearing. He also refused to slap and pop strings, which was what all the producers and arrangers wanted out there on their recordings."

Jamerson was also running into problems because of his habit of using old, dead strings. The new recording techniques offered a much broader spectrum of bass sounds to the listener, and consequently placed new demands on the players and their instruments. The fat, round tone that was so essential to the Detroit Motown sound was being replaced by a tighter and more defined bass sound on the West Coast. James' crusty five-year-old flat wound strings were not making it. Arranger Gene Page recounts, "Somewhere in the mid-to-late seventies, I called him for a date and he played really well, but he had an intonation problem. I thought that this was really strange because with all the great facility that he had, you wouldn't expect a pitch problem. I talked to Nathan East and he told me that it was because he wouldn't change those old strings. They weren't made to hold up that long."

Around the same time, James had been booked to play the original version of "Lady" for Lionel Ritchie, but wound up being scratched from the session for similar intonation and tone problems. Studio guitar wizard Paul Jackson Jr., who was also on the date, felt so bad that he ran out and bought James a box of round wound strings to help him modernize his sound. James was appreciative, but the strings never left the plastic wrapping.

A perfect example of the state of Jamerson's bass playing in the late seventies is a 1978 Bonnie Pointer track called "Heaven Must Have Sent You." With the exception of a few momentary timing problems, Jamerson flirts with some of the brilliance of his mid-sixties masterpieces. It's almost like listening to some of the final recordings of Arthur Rubinstein or Andres Segovia, during which the brief visions of the glory of their youth make you forget the technical flaws of their declining years. But as good as Jamerson's bass playing is on this record, it sounds out of place in comparison to the contemporary tone of the other bassist on the rest of the album. James' track is mixed way out in front, and it's easy to hear that the engineer was doing his best to somehow modernize the sound coming out of his dead strings.

According to James Jr., his father could have met the new stylistic and technical demands that were being placed on him, but he just didn't want to. "Imagine if someone had come up to Dizzy Gillespie, or Jimi Hendrix, or some other musician who had invented a style of playing, and said to them, 'Hey man, I want you to stop playing the way you've been playing all your life and try to sound like everybody else.' See, they were telling my Dad to stop being James Jamerson and there was no way that was ever going to happen." Robert White adds, "I think that he was so good at what he did that he did not change with the times. He was so proud that he wouldn't borrow from the new trends. He thought his trend would last forever."

Martha Reeves visiting her old friend at his home in California.

As the eighties approached, it started to become apparent to everyone that James was not going to return from the self-destructive path he had chosen. Alcohol was no longer something that he struggled with. It was now a runaway train that was completely out of control. Worst of all, the happy-go-lucky attitude and positive

The Fall of the King

outlook that had carried him through all the tribulations of his life, were now replaced by self-pity and hopelessness.

Watching his health and talents slip away was extremely traumatic for his family. James was going through a self-flagellation period during which he would listen to old Motown records that he had played on. He rarely got through more than a few minutes before he would break down and cry while muttering to himself, "I did it, I did it." It was as if James was trying to convince himself that at one time, he *was* the king of the bass world. According to Paul Riser, this type of behavior was typical during his last year. "He kept trying to live in the past. His mind always took him back to the good times and why it couldn't still be that way."

"His biggest downfall," says Frank Wilson, "was the fact that he spent all of those years being responsible for so much greatness in the record industry, and for whatever reason, he couldn't hold on to it. Out here he was in a much larger world. In Detroit, he *was* the world. When his career started to slow down, he found himself having financial challenges, and had a difficult time accepting that he was not rolling in the money while a lot of other people were doing extremely well. If he could have held on, he would have ended up being on a $100,000 to $150,000 retainer in L.A., because they eventually ended up putting musicians out here on retainer who were working with the corporation. Ironically, the idea spawned from the fact that Jamerson was originally on retainer. The bitterness began to eat away at him. It was always Motown. I never heard him say that he was to blame."

Annie agrees with Frank and says, "For years, he had played high and he just couldn't accept that his body would no longer allow him to do that. He was looking for a scapegoat. I won't lay any heavy blame on Motown. Maybe things could have been different, but my husband hurt himself by the inception of his disease."

Earl Van Dyke had known that something was definitely wrong when he saw James throw his bass on the floor during a late seventies recording session. The rest of the Funk Brothers caught on shortly after when Earl, Eddie Bongo, Robert White, and James were reunited for a 1979 record date in Los Angeles. As Robert recalls, "It was a nostalgia kind of thing where somebody wanted the original Motown feel. It was a great get-together— just like old home week. There was a lot of love in the place, but Jamerson was only a shadow of himself. Someone had taken his heart and his killer instinct. He was very passive—almost like he had a frontal lobotomy."

Paul Riser and Smokey Robinson had similar experiences with James on a few sessions that occurred late in his career. Paul recalls, "The last session I ever had with Jamerson, I tried to get him to find the downbeat on this tune we were working on, but he never found it. It was the weirdest experience I ever had. He kept feeling the downbeat on the upbeat." On Smokey's session, Jamerson was hired to play on a disco remake of "Get Ready," but Robinson's initial excitement of working with his old bass player quickly turned to melancholy when

Jamerson gave this photo to James Jr. and said, "Son, when this picture was taken, I was gittin' it."

he saw what had become of his abilities. "It was a real bad experience for me," laments Smokey, "because he couldn't even play the basic line that he had recorded years before. It was like: he was once a champion boxer, and now here he is matched with a bum, and the bum knocks him out. It was like watching Muhammed Ali getting beat up in some of his last fights. It hurt me to have to watch it."

James' diminishing talents could no longer be solely blamed on the medication that he was taking. His technique was originally cultivated through thousands of hours of recording and performing, but since he was never the type of musician who would practice at home, the radical dropoff in his career caused his chops to atrophy from lack of use. To further aggravate the situation, James had an artery severed when he was stabbed in the right arm during a 1981 mugging incident. Still, an occasional session would roll in, but people were beginning to treat him as a novelty. Whether his style was right for the material these acts were recording was inconsequential. They just wanted his name on their album and the experience of cutting with a legend. James saw the writing on the wall one afternoon when both he and James Jr. were accidentally booked on the same session. When they met at the studio and realized what had happened, James tearfully hugged his son and said, "Go in there and kick ass." On that day, the dream of "Jamerson & Son" monopolizing the West Coast studio scene officially died.

In the final two years of James Jamerson's life, his health, his marriage, and his career were withering away. Much of this period was spent in and out of hospitals and mental health centers, but it's a fitting testimonial to the true essence of the man that the last lingering sign of Jamerson's glory days was not his music, but his benevolence and kindness. His last few months were occupied with producing a young singer-songwriter named Kenny Koontz. As Koontz recalls, "With all his problems, he was still trying to help out everybody else. In the neighborhood, if he saw a kid going astray, he would sit him down and talk to him. He was like the Godfather of the block. I remember when my grandmother died, I was depressed because I didn't have enough money to fly out for her funeral, which was in Texas. James just looked at me and said, 'Get in the car,' and he drove me over 2000 miles roundtrip." "He was the same way in the hospitals," says Annie. "He would be running around helping out everyone else, and he was so proud of it. I told him maybe he ought to think about helping himself a little bit."

Ironically, the last song that Jamerson ever played bass on was a Kenny Koontz composition called "L.A. is the Place." In James' case, he should have retitled it,

James posing with Stevie Wonder and his friend and former Motown producer, Frank Wilson.

The Fall of the King

"L.A. is *Not* the Place." "My father would still be alive today if he had never moved there," glumly states James Jr. "He should have never left Detroit." In his final days, as it turned out, a welcome visit from some of James' old hometown friends would be his last link with any semblance of happiness. Eddie Willis and Eddie "Bongo" Brown were the last Funk Brothers to see him before he died. Willis remembers:

"I was in L.A. with the Four Tops, and at the time, I would always get in contact with Bongo and James when I came through town. Bongo and I went to visit him 'cause we had heard he wasn't doing too well. He was in bed and was very, very thin. He didn't look too much like James anymore. When we walked in, he started crying because he was so thrilled to see us. Bongo went outside; he couldn't take it. He said to me, 'This guy won't make it three more days.'"

Eddie Bongo wasn't too far off with his prediction. James was going down quickly. As a final insult to his once indomitable spirit, the 1962 Fender Precision, which had been his friend and companion for the previous twenty-one years, was stolen from his house. On August 1, 1983, within a few days of this incident, Annie came home to find James slumped over on the bed. The following evening on August 2 at 9:00 P.M., James Jamerson passed away at USC County Hospital of complications stemming from cirrhosis of the liver, heart failure, and pneumonia. His last words were an expression of concern for the welfare of his children.

CODA

It is a bright, sunny morning in Los Angeles, and Annie Jamerson sits in her living room, alone with her thoughts. It has been almost two weeks since her husband's funeral services. At churches in both Detroit and Los Angeles, more than 600 people had paid their last respects to James. Annie had sat through hours of eulogies and performances by some of the world's most celebrated Rhythm and Blues musicians and singers, but at this moment, her only desire is to escape into the peace and serenity of the dawn. As she stares out her bay window while listening to some old Motown records that James played on, she feels a small bead of water gently splash onto her hand. Looking down, she observes the tear-shaped droplet trickle down towards her fingers, and out of nowhere, she hears a voice in her head gently saying, "Sorry."

Not one to believe in spirits or ghosts, she immediately gets up to investigate the source of this precipitation but her efforts are fruitless. The plants near her are dry as a bone, and there are no apparent leaks in the ceiling. Thinking that perhaps she had inadvertently been crying, she walks to a mirror to find that her eyes are also completely dry. After a fleeting moment of anxiety, a warm sense of tranquility sweeps through her soul, and she sits back down to enjoy her husband's bass playing and the warmth of the morning sun.

While this may sound like a scene out of a Harlequin Romance novel, five years later in 1988, Annie is still haunted by that experience. "Perhaps," as she explained to me, "it was James apologizing for what he put me and the kids through in the later years." Of course, it could also be the overactive imagination of a grieving widow, but while James may have hypothetically felt the need to ask forgiveness from his family, there was certainly never any need for him to apologize for his music or his career. Although some may say that, "He had it all but couldn't hold on to it," keep in mind that James accomplished more in his decade and a half with Motown than most musicians could accomplish in ten lifetimes.

Many of the people I interviewed insisted that James Jamerson *was* "the Motown Sound," but this would be an unfair and untrue position to take. Everyone from Berry Gordy on down to the people who worked in the record shipping department was essential to this musical phenomenon. But consider this: As great as Martha and the Vandellas, Holland-Dozier-Holland, Marvin Gaye, and all the other Motown stars and production teams were, they *only* worked on the Motown records that they specifically wrote, produced or performed on. When David Ruffin sang "My Girl," Diana Ross was nowhere to be seen or heard, and when Valerie Simpson and Nick Ashford wrote and produced "Ain't Nothing Like The Real Thing," Smokey Robinson wasn't even in the building.

Annie Jamerson photographed in 1988 outside of Hitsville U.S.A.

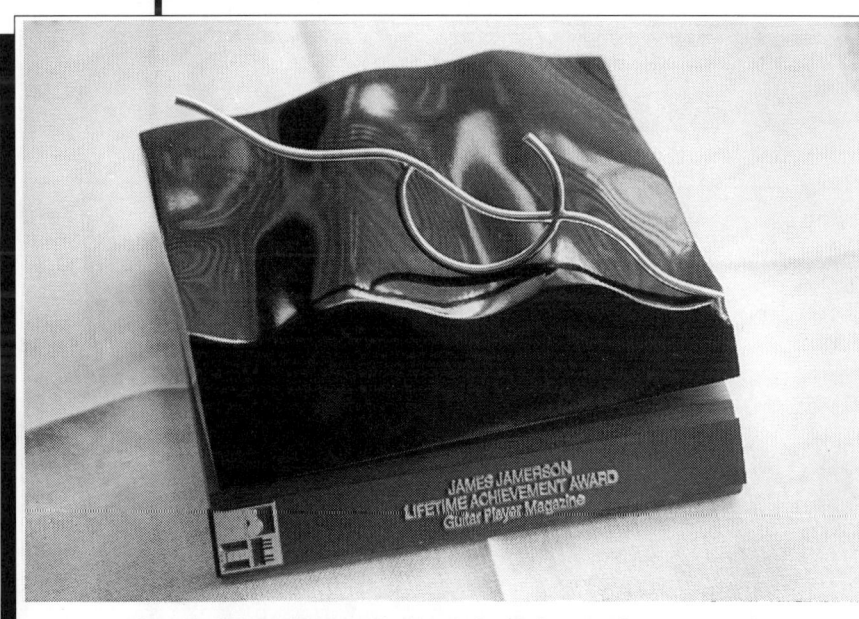

The Lifetime Achievement Award posthumously presented to James Jamerson by *Guitar Player*.

Coda

But during the heyday of Motown, James played on almost every record—regardless of producer, songwriter, arranger, or artist.

Today, the magical grooves that James and the Funk Brothers created down in the Snakepit stand alone in a unique musical category. They are not Funk, Rock, or Rhythm and Blues, or even "Oldies"—they are Motown. No matter how many times you listen to them, they sound just as fresh and vital today as they originally did when they blasted out of sixties' juke boxes. And the lifeblood of all of them is not just James Jamerson's bass playing . . . it is James Jamerson's heart.

The next time you're driving in your car and a vintage Motown track comes on the radio, as hard as this may sound, try to tune out the vocals of Stevie Wonder, or Diana Ross, or Levi Stubbs for just a little while, and focus in on James Jamerson's bass part. Then try to imagine how the same music would sound without it. The vocals would still be great, but it just wouldn't be "The Same Old Song" anymore.

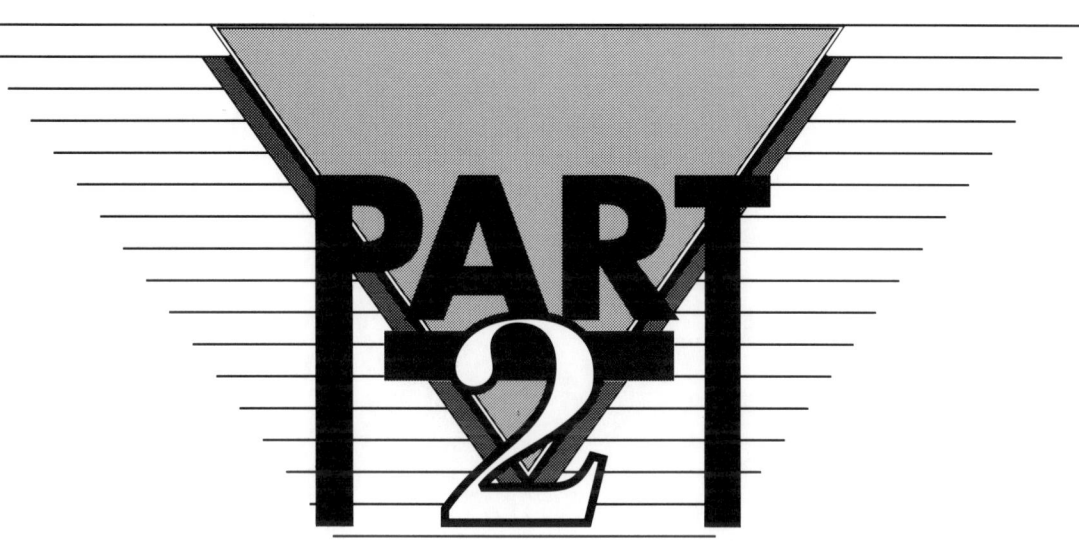

Anatomy of a Sound

80

ANATOMY OF A SOUND

"The Snakepit" Part II. Notice the big monitor speaker to the right of the steps that James and all the guitarists listened to when cutting tracks.

A conversation with Mike McClain can often turn into a full scale dissertation on vacuum tube theory, signal to noise ratios, and magnetic flux density. Mike is the mad scientist who built and maintained the recording equipment that captured the magic of Motown's musicians and singers. But his electronic creations were much more than just sponges that absorbed everyone else's ideas so that they could be reproduced on vinyl. They played an indispensable role in the overall Motown Sound, and James Jamerson's bass sound in particular.

Shortly after arriving at Motown in 1961, Mike began to make plans to upgrade their two-track facility. Working around the clock for three days with $1500 worth of spare parts, Mike overhauled the recording console and added a third channel that made its debut on the Marvelettes' 1962 smash, "Please Mr. Postman." Two years later, completely by-passing 4-track technology, which had become the rage of the music industry, Mike made a quantum leap to eight tracks for the Supremes' "Baby Love" session. From this point on, Jamerson's bass would assume a more prominent role in the Motown mixes. With five additional tracks, the engineers could now reserve one track for James' bass all by itself. The

The control booth at Hitsville U.S.A. as it appeared almost twenty-five years ago. (There aren't too many candy machines in the control booths nowadays.)

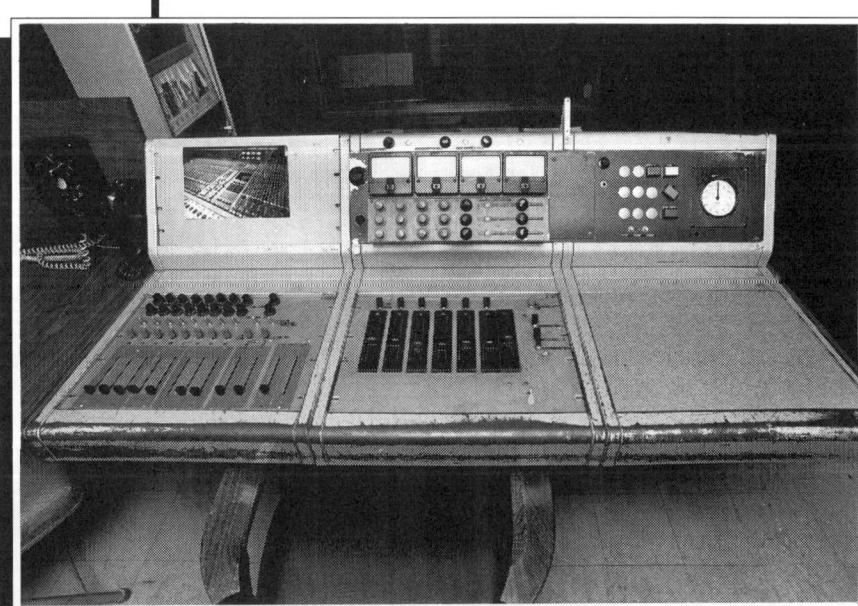
In this close-up of Motown's early recording console, check out the picture of the half-a-million dollar SSL console that some prankster taped to the left of the VU meters.

indistinct bottom end of the early recordings, which resulted from sandwiching him in amongst all the other instruments, was now eliminated.

However, it wasn't just additional tracks that made Motown's recordings sound so much different from the rest of the pop world. "The engineering had a lot to do with the sound," explains Hank Cosby. "One of the secrets of the Motown Sound was this rolling-spinning echo that they had. It was a home made unit." In addition, procedural innovations in the recording process, and the acoustical qualities of the tiny room itself, with its wood floor and homemade isolation booths, produced a warmth and crispness unequaled in the larger and more sophisticated studios of New York and Chicago. The sound produced by this room was valued so highly by Motown, that they considered dismantling the entire setup, and then reassembling it in Los Angeles when they migrated there in the early seventies.

Because of the limited size of the Snakepit, and the inherent problems of live instruments bleeding into each others' mikes, Jamerson and the guitarists rarely recorded through amplifiers. All the electronic instruments went directly into the recording console. Mike McClain remembers, "Under the control booth window on the wall, was a five instrument interface panel with variable gain controls and VU meters. Jamerson and the guitar players would plug into this unit and then use the Bozak monitor speaker next to the steps to hear themselves. Each guy was responsible for setting his own level and controlling how much mush they wanted in their sound, by adjusting the gain control and the VU meter."

The "mush" that Mike refers to was an essential element of Jamerson's fat, round tone. By adjusting his volume so that it was slightly hotter than acceptable levels on the VU meter, James was able to overdrive the tubes in the recording console and create a slight amount of distortion that rounded out his sound. From that point, the engineers would usually tailor his sound a bit more by adding a Fairchild limiter (an electronic device that softens overly loud passages and keeps them from sticking out in the mix) and one or two Pultec equalizers.

These relatively simple recording procedures are dwarfed by today's advanced studio technology, but progress isn't always better when art is involved. Even though Jamerson's West Coast career of the seventies and eighties would lead him to record at vastly superior sixteen and twenty-four track facilities, his tone was never more lush and vibrant than in the days of Hitsville's old eight-track operation.

B-15's AND FUNK MACHINES

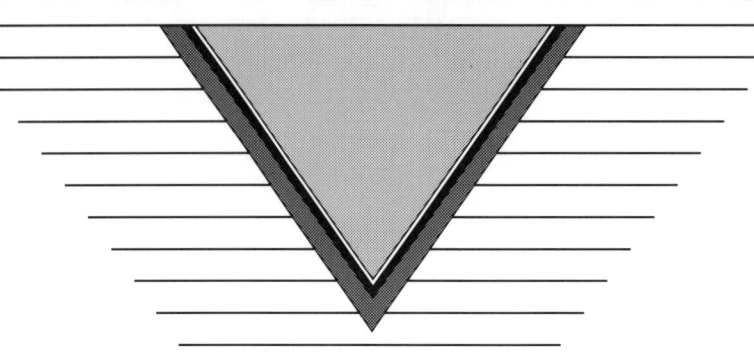

It has become commonplace in the eighties for studio musicians to own a full arsenal of instruments. The constantly changing musical demands that are placed on modern day session players necessitate having different types of instruments to meet each new trend as it comes along. James Jamerson was never comfortable in this environment because he never chased trends—he made them. Besides, when producers hired James to play on their sessions, they were usually looking for "the Jamerson Sound," and not "the Soul Train Bass Sound of the Week." The instruments that James chose to play, and his deep emotional involvement with them, were direct results of his artistic convictions. He had a very specific sound in his head that was not altered by the fickle currents and fads of the pop music world; consequently, the instruments that he felt were essential for producing this sound did not change either. If not for thievery, Jamerson would have probably played his entire career on one upright and one electric bass.

James' first bass was loaned to him by his high school—it wasn't exactly a Stradivarius. James friend, Richard "Popcorn" Wylie, described it as "a big upright bass that had a body that was made out of tin." When James graduated in 1957, he purchased a German bass which was the only upright that he would ever own during his lifetime. The incredibly stiff action and high string height had a lot to do with the strength of his hands, and the way that he would set up his electric basses in later years. This upright was always James' first love. The thousands of hours that he spent playing on it are reflected by the 1/4 inch indentation on the side of the fingerboard, at the spot where his right thumb rested.

Up until 1960, Jamerson played upright exclusively at all his live and studio dates. He eventually installed a makeshift pickup on it, but he had no intention of switching over to a solid body electric bass until his friend, Horace "Chili" Ruth, persuaded him to make the transition. "I was trying to turn him on to the Fender bass," says Chili. "We started switching basses and I would use his upright and he would use my Fender, and then we'd meet up after our gigs. I told him, 'You can always go back to the upright, but things are changing and you should switch over and get an electric bass.' He said he didn't want to do that and I said, 'Well OK, I'm gonna buy me another one anyway so you can have 'the Black Beauty' (a refinished '57 Fender Precision). He said, 'Well in that case, I'll buy it.' Later on, he said that it was the sweetest thing that he ever did."

Robbery plagued James throughout his musical career. The '57 Precision didn't last very long. It was eventually stolen from the trunk of his car, as was the early sixties sunburst Precision that he bought to replace it. This set the stage for the purchase of the bass that would accompany Jamerson into musical history. Until the last few weeks of his life, when it too was stolen, this instrument never left his side. Earl Van Dyke made me aware of the reverence with which Motown studio musicians regarded that particular bass. Dur-

Jamerson's German upright bass.

ing the course of my interview with Earl, I informed him that it had been stolen. Following a few seconds of horrified silence, Earl moaned, "Oh no! Not The Funk Machine! Not The Funk Machine!"

"The Funk Machine," as James and the rest of the Funk Brothers called it, had probably produced more hits than any bass in the history of the recording industry. There was nothing extraordinary about it. It was a stock '62 sunburst Fender Precision with the bell, the metal centerpiece, and foam mute all intact. Jamerson never removed them as he felt they were an integral part of the instrument's sound and balance. The only part of the instrument that wasn't stock was the heel of the neck, where James had carved the word "Funk" into the wood and filled it in with blue ink.

The unique sound that Jamerson got out of his bass had a lot to do with the way it was set up. For starters, the foam mute was usually pressed against the strings, and the string height was extremely high, which accounts for the absence of fret buzzing on any of James' recorded tracks. The neck was also bowed a bit because the truss rod was not sufficiently tightened. Musicians who had the chance to try out his bass usually found it to be almost unplayable, but for James it was fine because of his unusual hand strength. The strings were exclusively heavy gauge Labella flat wounds that usually weren't changed unless they broke. It wasn't uncommon for Jamerson to be playing with strings that were several years old.

As far as maintenance, Jamerson would occasionally polish or clean his bass, but he never touched the fingerboard. "Dad used to tell me, 'The dirt keeps the funk,'" explains James Jr. "If you saw the last bass, there was a lot of buildup on the neck and strings from the years of playing. It looked funky, like it had been through a battlefield. It had been dropped a lot of different times."

On a few rare sessions, James experimented a bit with a Hagstrom 8-string, an early Fender 5-string, and a fretless bass, but the end results were usually unsatis-

An essential element of "the Jamerson Sound"—heavy guage Labella flatwound strings.

The Fender 5 string.

factory. (Earl Van Dyke recalled that James played the fretless on the Supremes' "Someday, We'll Be Together" and almost threw it against the wall at the end of the session screaming, "Don't you ever let me play this piece of shit again.") The Hagstrom bass was eventually stolen in Los Angeles.

At home, Jamerson also played around with some effects pedals, but never cared for them because he felt that they diminished the bass quality of the instrument.

James had two basic amplifier setups. For clubs and concerts in smaller venues, he used an Ampeg B-15 (guess what also eventually happened to this?) with an occasional extension cabinet. For large halls, he used a blue padded Kustom amplifier with two 15" speakers. Both amps were set with the bass knob all the way up and the treble control on half. His Fender bass was always set with the volume and tone controls all the way up.

Unfortunately, the Jamerson family today only possesses the upright bass, the Fender five string, and James' Kustom amp. The strings on the basses and the tone and volume controls on the amp haven't been changed since James was alive. In fact, the gunk that had built up on the necks from years of sweating away in studios and clubs, still remains on the fingerboards as a ghostly reminder of the genius who once played them. Perhaps one of the biggest tragedies of Jamerson's story is that someone out there probably has no idea that the beat-up 1962 Fender Precision that they own was once proudly called, "the Funk Machine."

Jamerson's sparkle blue Kustom amplifier.

THE CAST

James would never throw a party without inviting his friends. The following is a listing of the prominent studio musicians who helped to create Hitsville's Studio Sound.

BASS
James Jamerson, Bob Babbitt, Michael Henderson, Eddie Watkins, Clarence Isabell, Prof. Beard, Joe James, Tony Newton

GUITARS
Eddie Willis, Robert White, Joe Messina, Wawa Watson, Dennis Coffey, Marv Tarplin, Cornelius Grant, Larry Veeder, Dave Hamilton

KEYBOARDS
Earl Van Dyke, Johnny Griffith, James Gittens, Joe Hunter, Richard "Popcorn" Wylie, Ted Sheely, Joe Weaver

DRUMS
Benny Benjamin, Uriel Jones, Richard "Pistol" Allen, George McGregor, Frederick Waites, Andrew Smith, Clifford Mack, Larry London

PERCUSSION and VIBES
Eddie "Bongo" Brown, Jack Brokensha, Jack Ashford, Dave Hamilton, James Gittens

TRUMPETS
Floyd Jones, John Trudell, John (Little John) Wilson, Herbie Williams

SAXOPHONES
Thomas "Beans" Bowles, Hank Cosby, Eli Fontaine, Andrew "Mike" Terry, Bernie Peacock, Lefty Edwards, Ronnie Wakefield, Norris Patterson, William "Wild Bill" Moore, Dan Turner, Teddy Bucker

TROMBONES
George Bohannon, Paul Riser, Bob Cousar, Carl Raetz, Patrick Lanier

FLUTES and REEDS
Dayna Hartwick, Thomas "Beans" Bowles

STRINGS
Gordon Staples (concertmaster) and the Detroit Symphony string section

ARRANGERS
Paul Riser, Willie Shorter, Dave Van DePitte, Wade Marcus, Hank Cosby, Jerry Long, Slide Hampton, Ernie Wilkins, Gil Askey, Johnny Allen

RECORDING ENGINEERS
Mike McClain, Lawrence Horn, Robert Bateman, Ed Red, Art Stewart, James Green

DISCOGRAPHY

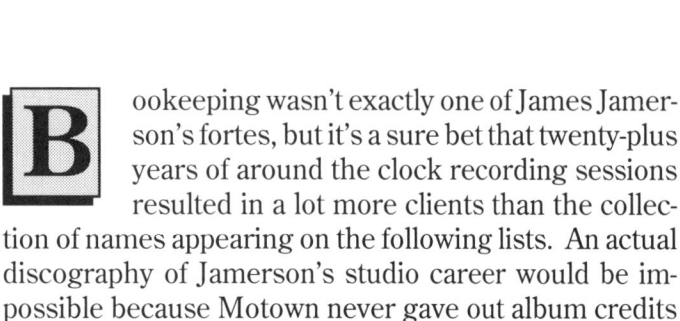

Bookkeeping wasn't exactly one of James Jamerson's fortes, but it's a sure bet that twenty-plus years of around the clock recording sessions resulted in a lot more clients than the collection of names appearing on the following lists. An actual discography of Jamerson's studio career would be impossible because Motown never gave out album credits until the seventies, and James never kept accurate records of his session work.

Referring to a massive anthology released by Motown several years back, critic Griel Marcus dubbed it, "James Jamerson's Greatest Hits." That may be the most accurate discography of all, because both Jamerson's and Motown's recorded outputs during the glory years of 1963 to 1968 are synonomous—James played on virtually every track. While his outside session work never approached the artistic heights of his Motown performances, Jamerson's contributions to the success of hundreds of other Pop, Rock, Folk, Jazz, Blues, and R&B albums were significant and deserve to be mentioned.

In an attempt to give some indication of the extent of his studio accomplishments, a list of substantiated acts that Jamerson recorded with (along with some selected albums) has been assembled. This compilation has been put together from the memories of his family, friends, fellow musicians, producers, and the massive pile of records in the basement of his home in Detroit. While this list is by no means complete, it should help to illustrate just how rich and diverse James Jamerson's recording career was.

Motown Acts

The Temptations, Eddie Kendricks, David Ruffin, Jimmy Ruffin, the Marvelettes, Smokey Robinson and the Miracles, the Supremes, Diana Ross, Mary Wells, Edwin Starr, Shorty Long, Marvin Gaye, Tammi Terrell, Kim Weston, the Isley Brothers, the Contours, Stevie Wonder, Martha and the Vandellas, the Velvelettes, Jr. Walker & the All-Stars, the Undisputed Truth, the Spinners, the Originals, Gladys Knight and the Pips, the Four Tops, the Elgins, Bonnie Pointer, Marv Johnson, the Twistin' Kings, Eddie Holland, Chris Clark, Billy Eckstine, Barabara McNair, Chuck Jackson, G.C. Cameron, Yvonne Fair, Willie Hutch, Thelma Houston, Earl Van Dyke and the Soul Brothers, Sammy Ward, Barrett Strong, Valerie Simpson, the Monitors, Choker Campbell, Caston and Majors, the Jackson Five, Chuck Jackson, Brenda Holloway

A Selective List of Jamerson Motown Albums

Gettin' Ready (The Temptations—Gordy)
My Guy (Mary Wells—Motown)
Reach Out (The Four Tops—Motown)
The Supremes Sing Holland-Dozier-Holland (The Supremes—Motown)
Home Cookin' (Jr. Walker and the All Stars—Soul)
I Was Made To Love Her (Stevie Wonder—Tamla)
Love Child (Diana Ross and the Supremes—Motown)
The Marvelous Marvelettes (The Marvelettes—Tamla)
You're All I Need To Get By (Marvin Gaye and Tammi Terrell—Tamla)
Away We A Go-Go (Smokey Robinson and the Miracles—Tamla)
Here Comes the Judge (Shorty Long—Soul)
What's Going On (Marvin Gaye-Tamla)
For Once In My Life (Stevie Wonder-Tamla)
Uptight (Stevie Wonder-Tamla)
With A Lot O' Soul (The Temptations-Gordy)
I Heard It Through The Grapevine (Marvin Gaye—Tamla)
Dance Party (Martha and the Vandellas—Gordy)

Non-Motown Acts and Projects

The Osmonds, Shirley Bassey, Joe Williams, Aretha Franklin, Joan Baez, Maria Muldaur, Yusef Lateef, Buddy Miles, Dennis Wilson, the Crusaders, the Mighty Clouds of Joy, Stanley Turrentine, Tom Jones, Charo, the Pointer Sisters, Nancy Wilson, Johnny Bristol, Curtis Mayfield, Jerry Butler, John Lee Hooker, J.J. Barnes, Johnnie Mae Matthews, James Darren, the Sandpipers, Hoyt Axton, the film score from Cooley High, the Starsky and Hutch TV theme, Houston Person, Willie Hutch, the S.W.A.T. TV theme, Jackie Wilson, the Hues Corporation, Al Green, the Dramatics, Robert Palmer, Marilyn McCoo and Billy Davis Jr., Jeff Beck, John Handy, Hugo Montenegro, Quincy Jones, Bill Withers, H.B. Barnum, Al Wilson, Bloodstone, Harvey Mason, the Caravans, the Sylvers

A Selective List of Jamerson Non-Motown Albums

I Heard That (Quincy Jones—A&M)
Instant Coffey (Dennis Coffey—Sussex)
Nobody Does It Like Me (Shirley Bassey—United Artists)
Rocket Man (Hugo Montenegro—RCA)
Carnival (John Handy—ABC)
Higher and Higher (Jackie Wilson—Brunswick)
The Power of Love (Jerry Butler—Mercury)
All the Faces of Buddy Miles (Buddy Miles—Columbia)
Having a Party (The Pointer Sisters—ABC)
Pressure Drop (Robert Palmer—Island)
Making Friends (Bill Withers—Columbia)
The Real Thing (Houston Person—Eastbound)
From Every Stage (Joan Baez—A&M)

IGOR'S CHROMATIC EXERCISE

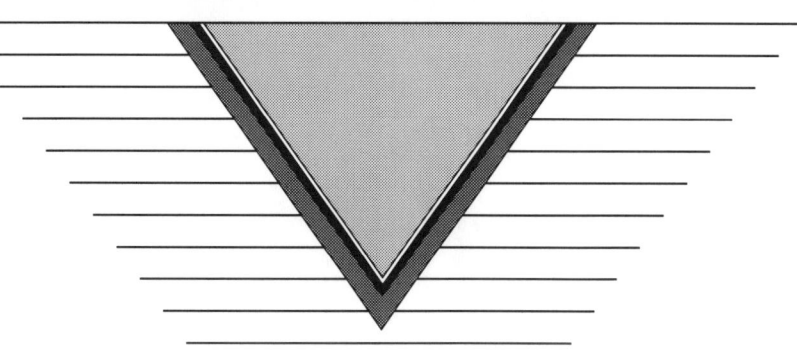

Discussing the effect that James Jamerson had on young bass players in the early seventies, producer Freddie Perren remembered, "On a lot of the West Coast Motown sessions, we used to use a guy named Ron Brown. He would come into the sessions with a stack of Jamerson transcriptions that he had written out from the records; and he would go over these charts before the session because he felt that it was the best way to get his head into the right frame of mind."

Ron also had the rare opportunity to "get his head in the right frame of mind" by having a few informal, one-on-one lessons with Jamerson. James showed him the exercise that appears below, and told Ron that he developed this etude to help him practice his chromatic approach to bass playing.

In keeping with Jamerson's preference for heavy bottom, he makes slight alterations in each four bar phrase as they go through the cycle of fifths. This way, he can remain in the open and lower positions and compensate at the same time for changes in range and open strings within each new key.

AN APPRECIATION OF THE STYLE

BY ANTHONY JACKSON

Perhaps one of the most fascinating observations to be made today regarding Motown—twenty years after the end of the company's "golden" period (1964-1969)—is the complete lack of a stylistic descendant. With the departures of James Jamerson, the Funk Brothers, and Holland-Dozier-Holland, along with the transfer of Motown's base of operations from Detroit to Los Angeles, the characteristic "Motown Sound" of the '60s quickly disappeared. Little attempt to perpetuate or develop the original sound appears to have been made; Motown made a clear cut decision to move on.

This leaves us with a rare example of a complete musical phenomenon observable from point of inception to dissipation. While a full analysis of "the Motown Sound" is beyond the scope of this book, the basics of James Jamerson's style (within the Motown context) should be examined in order to fully understand the transcriptions featured in Part III. Even though the material presented here only scratches the surface of the subject, it should serve as a good foundation for further study (in conjunction with the transcriptions and the original tracks). My intent here is to identify and explain a few key elements of Jamerson's revolutionary bass concept, through a brief analysis of three important Motown recordings:

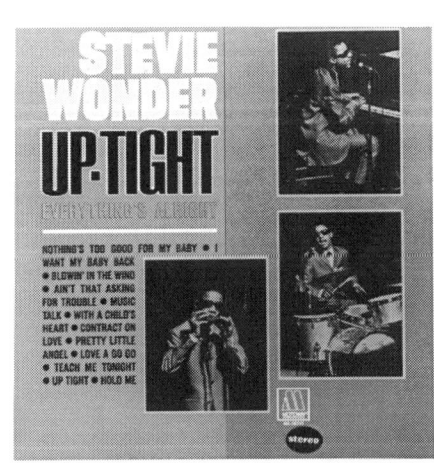

"Uptight
(Everything's Alright)"
from the 1966 Stevie Wonder album,
UPTIGHT

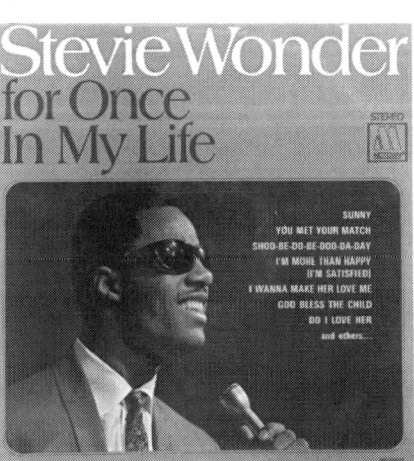

"I'd Be A
Fool Right Now"
from the 1968 Stevie Wonder album,
FOR ONCE IN MY LIFE

"How Long Has That
Evening Train Been Gone"
from the 1968 Supremes album,
LOVE CHILD

"UPTIGHT (EVERYTHING'S ALRIGHT)"
(Words and Music by Stevie Wonder, Sylvia Moy, and Hank Cosby)

Harmonic and Rhythmic Ambiguity

The implied 2 bar motif used in "Uptight"—certainly one of the most popular among bass players of the '60s—became a unique and compelling creation in the hands of Jamerson. The boldness of his approach on this tune was unheard of at the time this track was recorded. Here are a few of the Jamerson techniques that helped to make "Uptight" the success that it was:

1) The use of anticipations to avoid downbeats—At the beginning of every 2nd bar of each two bar phrase, the downbeat is non-existent, having been carried over from the 4+ of the previous bar. The basic timekeeping quality of the pocket is therefore left to the snare drum, which is playing quarter notes. The bass now assumes a more subtle timekeeping quality.

2) Using right-hand touch sensitivity to alter rhythmic feel—Where downbeats do occur in this example, emphasis is often at points other than those downbeat because of Jamerson's variations in attack. For example, at the start of every two bar phrase, the Db is usually attacked lightly. The emphasis is actually on the F at beat two.

3) The bold use of the passing tone to redefine harmonic structure—The Gb anticipation leading into bar 8 would normally be quickly resolved to an Ab in order to eventually lead to the Db (the home tonality) in bar 9. Jamerson, however, hangs on the Gb for a full beat and a half, giving it an emphasis it would not normally have. By maintaining the note this long, the result is the perception of a new harmonic structure. The surrounding harmony now relates to the Gb as a tonic note, resulting in a most unusual harmonic flavor.

The two bar phrase at bars 19 and 20 contains one of the boldest variations on this technique. The G natural—seen previously on beat two of most even numbered bars—is now moved to beat three in bar 20, where it no longer strictly functions as a passing tone. Its location at this point, combined with its emphasis in the attack, creates a powerful dissonance against the existing Cb/Db harmony. This is quickly relieved by the move to Ab on beat 4, and the eventual resolution to Db in bar 21. Again, a classic example of tension-and-release.

"I'D BE A FOOL RIGHT NOW"
(Words and Music by Stevie Wonder, Hank Cosby, and Sylvia Moy)

Use of Contrasts in Phrasing for Motivic Development
This bass part is a masterful example of extremes and compositional maturity.

1) Abrupt transitions between busy, dynamic motion and inactive, sustained passages—A combination of abrupt starts and stops sets the tone for the verse in this example. The aggressive staccato figure in measure 3 of the intro comes to an abrupt halt on the downbeat of measure four, which is a sustained half note. The actual verse, beginning at measure 5, reverses the pattern of frenetic motion followed by sustained notes. In bar 5, we see a strong quarter note standing alone. This is followed by a rather busy phrase leading into the next bar, where we again land on a strong isolated quarter note. At this point, another busy phrase leads into bar 7, and so on until bar 8, where this pattern is broken. Once again, the drums provide rhythmic smoothness and consistency, allowing the bass to have its way.

2) Abrupt transitions between horizontal and vertical motion—Jamerson's utilization of linear scale development in bars 5 through 7 instantly shifts gears at bar 8 with a stunning two octave arpeggio that appears without warning. Following the low open E at the end of the arpeggio, he immediately leaps up to a high Db and resumes scalar motion. This intimidating display of dexterity in bar 8 is accomplished at a brisk tempo (with absolute control) in the space of only three beats.

3) Numerous and unexpected changes of melodic direction in short amounts of time—In bars 5 and 6, in the space of only eight beats, Jamerson heightens melodic interest by reversing direction six times.

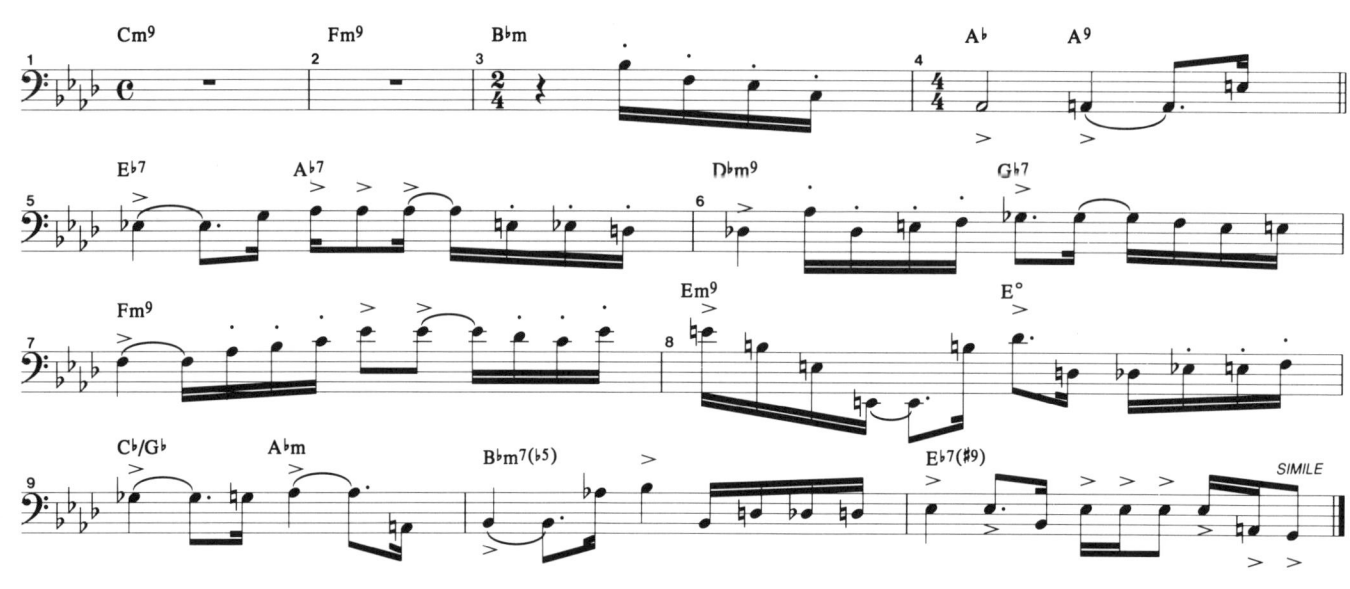

"HOW LONG HAS THAT EVENING TRAIN BEEN GONE"
(Words and Music by Frank Wilson and Pam Sawyer)

Selective Use of Dissonance as an Effect
The boldness of Jamerson's innovations are highlighted in this Supremes track. This excerpt is loaded with examples of non-diatonicism that Jamerson somehow managed to use to his advantage.

1) The use of unstable harmonic and melodic connecting phrases—Groups of notes that link harmonic target areas. These phrases often exhibit jagged distortions in scalar direction, and harmonic discontinuity, making them sound "wrong." These "wrong" passages create astonishing tension-and-release within the song, heightening the emotional development. Superficial analysis, prompting one to "correct" these passages, would result in the complete collapse of the bass part's impact.

In measure 5, what would be a standard Eb7 motif leading to the Ab7sus in bar 6, is cleverly altered by the continual appearance of an A natural (a tritone in the key of Eb, and clearly a "wrong" note). This overall dissonance against the tonality of the bar, combined with numerous scalar direction changes leading up to bar 6, yields a fine example of the harmonic and melodic "edge" in Jamerson's style.

2) The use of "lazy" open strings—Originally conceived, no doubt, to facilitate position shifts, this technique evolved into an essential element of the Jamerson style. This is probably the most misunderstood characteristic of his approach. Referring back to the "wrong" A naturals in bars 5 through 7, these are all open strings. Jamerson loved to use this technique in keys like Ab, Gb, Eb and Db, where the open strings were notes out of the key. This technique requires the open string to be attacked, and the following fretted note on the next lower string to be plucked using the same stroke. This is sometimes referred to as a "rake."

3) Approaching chordal roots by non-diatonic half step motion—With the exception of the C natural at the end of bar 6, leading into the D flat at the beginning of bar 7, all of the first notes of each new chord change in bars 5 through 8 are approached by a non-diatonic half-step. This technique is very common in many of Jamerson's recordings, and may have come from his jazz background.

Perhaps the key word that sums up the techniques presented in this chapter, and Jamerson's style in general, is "unpredictability." It was impossible to foresee what he would play. Former Motown bassist, Ron Brown, perfectly described this facet of Jamerson's approach when he said:

"He had a unique ability to set your ear up in terms of listening to music. Like a rider on a horse, it would be like . . . he'd start you off at a nice galloping pace and race down the track; and all of a sudden, he'd take a right turn and throw you and you'd be out flying in space not knowing where you are. Then just before you touch the earth, he's right back there and you land in the saddle. You see, he had the ability to suggest to your ear where he wanted you to think that he was going . . . but then he wouldn't go there. But then somehow, he'd always manage to wind up back on his feet when beat one came around."

An Appreciation of The Jamerson Style

In this close-up of James Jamerson's hand position, you can see his one-fingered approach. His pinky, middle, and ring fingers are anchored on the bell (the metal centerpiece), and his thumb is hanging freely. James called his index finger, "The Hook."

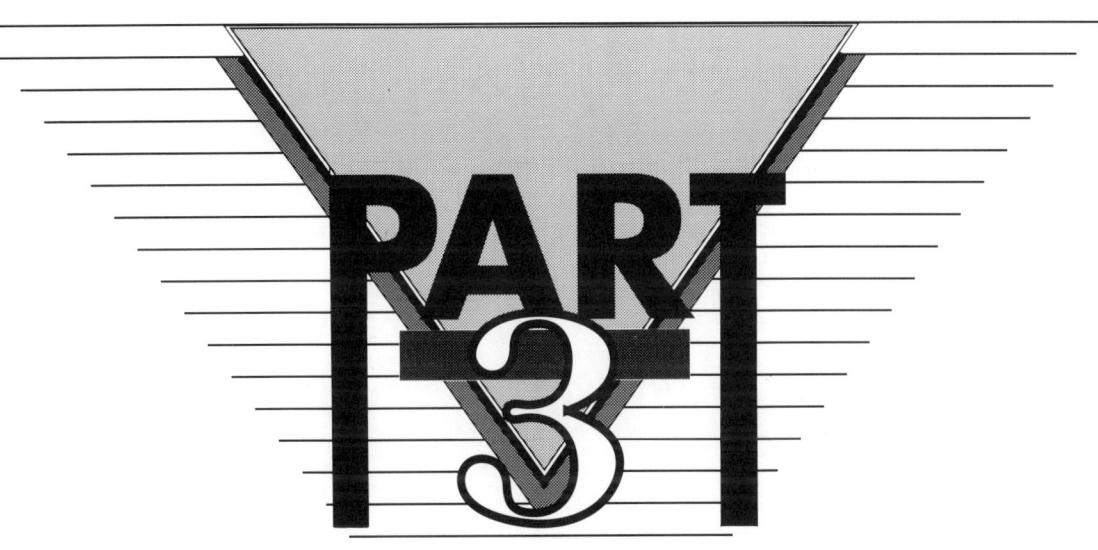

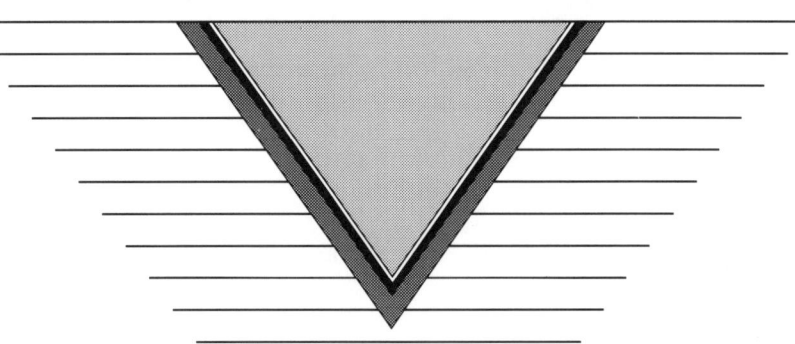

STARS AND SCORES

I have always felt that words are a completely inadequate medium for describing or commenting on music. Unfortunately, language is still the human race's primary source of communication, since we have not yet evolved to the stage where we are all mind readers. That's why this book has one great advantage over most texts dealing with musical subjects; accompanying this book are two cassettes that feature 25 world famous bassists making both verbal, and more appropriately, musical statements that explain what James Jamerson's music was all about. It saves me the agony of having to write things like, "Jamerson's bass lines on 'Bernadette' were played with great panache and flair," . . . or some other useless comment.

How did it come to pass that all of these musicians, who are accustomed to earning double and triple session scale (and often more), agreed to play on these tapes for free? Believe me, it's not because of my winning smile or my salesmanship. The ease with which most of the stars were recruited is a strong testimonial to the esteem and regard that the music world has for James Jamerson. Most of the musicians I approached were more than eager to offer their time and talents to help honor the man who, in many cases, was one of the main reasons that they took up the bass in the first place.

Each of the guest artists chose one or more of Jamerson's bass parts from the list of transcriptions that I had available, and then recreated them in local studios or at their homes, using their own recording equipment. Although some of the contributing artists handled all aspects of the recording process on their respective performances, in most cases, a click-track and bass part were sent back and the background tracks were recreated in Philadelphia. (Some of the sessions were a bit more spontaneous, like the evening I caught Geddy Lee a few hours before a Rush concert at the Philadelphia Spectrum. He recorded his bass part right in the dressing room, with a cassette portastudio.) All of the performances are intended to be informal and conversational—almost as if the bassist is sitting down with the reader and saying, "Hey, check out what Jamerson did on this tune."

Most people know the big stars on the tape like Jack Bruce, Marcus Miller, and John Entwistle, but there are also a few names sprinkled throughout the tape that may not be quite as familiar. These musicians were chosen for a very specific reason: aside from selecting them because of their talents and recording credentials, I felt that it would be hypocritical to restrict the contributions to only famous stars. After all, James Jamerson was not exactly what you would call a "famous star." He was a sideman—and since this is a story about a sideman—a "behind the scenes type of musician," it's only fitting that other players in the same field should have some input.

About the transcriptions . . .

Some of the songs demand a virtuoso technique in order to perform them correctly, while others can be played by bassists who are on beginner and intermediate levels.

In either case, be aware that the feel is equally as important as the notes. Since this is one attribute of Jamerson's style that cannot be written out, it is highly recommended that you try and obtain some of the Motown albums that were the sources of these transcriptions, so that you can listen to what James' soul did with the notes. The album that each transcription came from is listed along with the song title. The charts appear in the same order as they are performed on the tapes.

While playing through the transcriptions, pay particular attention to the X's, which indicate muted notes (usually deadened open strings), and to the small O's, indicating open strings. These techniques are essential to the performance of Jamerson's lines. Some of the passages may stretch your ears a bit but remember; Jamerson's style was extremely chromatic—he often used dissonance and non-diatonic material as an effect. In addition, the occasional mistakes that James played on some of the original recordings are included in the transcriptions—I wouldn't dare correct them.

About the tapes . . .

When you listen to the cassettes for the first time, you may notice that all of the recorded songs have a very strange mix—the bass is all alone on the left channel, and all the other instruments are essentially a mono-mix on the right channel. This was done for a variety of reasons:

1) The focus of these tracks is the bass line, so the mono-mix isolates Jamerson's bass as the solo instrument.

2) It allows you to play engineer and mix in as much, or as little bass as you desire, by simply adjusting the balance control on your stereo. For example, If you want to hear the bass all by itself, turn your balance adjustment all the way to the left and the right channel (the instrumental background track) will disappear. For Motown fans who are not used to isolating specific instruments when they are listening to music, this is invaluable as it offers them the opportunity to hear what James actually did on the original recordings without the distractions of other instruments and vocals.

3) Bassists who want to play the transcriptions have a ready made backing track for a music-minus-one situation. All you have to do is turn your balance control all the way to the right and you will hear just a rhythm section with no bass. To focus in on a particularly tricky bass passage, you may want to hear the bass all by itself without having the interference of kick drums and other instruments in the same frequency range. To do this, just turn the balance knob of your stereo all the way to the left.

TAPE CONTENTS

TAPE ONE—SIDE A

- Paul McCartney
- James Jamerson Jr.
- Will Lee
- "Chili" Ruth and Joe Weaver
- John Entwistle
- Gerald Veasley
- Phil Chen
- Martha Reeves
- Pino Palladino
- Geddy Lee
- Joe Messina

TAPE ONE—SIDE B

- Chuck Rainey
- Wah Wah Watson
- The Philadelphia Intl. Rhythm Section
- Joe Hunter
- "Ready" Freddy Washington
- Garry Tallent
- Dennis Coffey
- Allen McGrier
- Gil Askey

TAPE TWO—SIDE A

- John Patitucci
- Gene Page
- Jimmy Haslip
- Bob Babbitt
- Robert White
- Willie Weeks
- Eddie Holland
- David Hungate
- Earl Van Dyke
- Francis Rocco Prestia
- Jack Bruce

TAPE TWO—SIDE B

- Kenny Aaronson
- Marcus Miller
- Nathan Watts
- Non-Motown Medley
- Basil Fearrington
- Smokey Robinson
- Anthony Jackson
- Brian Holland
- Stevie Wonder

PAUL McCARTNEY

*H*i there...

I'm very honored to have been asked to MC the introduction to this James Jamerson memorial tape. I'm honored for a couple of reasons: mainly because his style of bass playing for Motown was one of my major influences when I was learning electric bass, and I know that a lot of the people who are playing and demonstrating his technique on this tape have also been influenced by him.

He's one of the greats so, LONG LIVE THE NAME OF JAMES JAMERSON, and I hope this project goes on to greater heights. It certainly deserves to. Cheers... thanks a lot. On with the motley!

—*Paul McCartney*—
May 1988, London

JAMES JAMERSON JR.

Living in the shadow of a legend is not the most enviable of situations for a young, aspiring musician. James Jamerson Jr. put himself on the hot seat when he took up the same instrument as his Dad, and although the comparisons have been inescapable, he has managed to create his own niche in the R&B and Pop music worlds. Just ask Janet Jackson, Bob Dylan, Aretha Franklin, Smokey Robinson, Philip Bailey, Sergio Franchii, Luciano Pavarotti, Denise Williams, the Jacksons, and about thirty other headliners with whom James has recorded and toured. They hired him because of how *he* played—not because of who his father was. When you listen to his lines, you can definitely hear the roots of his style; the round, fat, bell-like tone is unmistakable. But James Jr. has also been able to take what his dad showed him and make it his own.

In one respect, James has even surpassed his "old man." Even though Jamerson Sr. wrote a few tunes and produced several artists, he was never able to break into the charts unless he was functioning as a sideman playing bass for someone else. But "Pops" was as proud as could be when his son's group, Chanson, hit the top ten with a song called "Don't Hold Back."

Today, James Jr. lives with his family in North Hollywood where he continues to pursue his studio and solo recording career, but he still finds time to get in some roadwork with acts like the Temptations, Laura Branigan, the Crusaders and Chaka Kahn.

Musicians' Credits on James Jamerson Jr.'s Tracks

Keyboards: Tim Heintz
Drum machine programming: Alvino Bennett
Additional keyboards: George Akerley
Live drums: Joe Nero
Guitar: Dr. Licks
Alto Sax: Ron Kerber
Arrangements transcribed by: Tim Heintz and Dr. Licks

What's Going On P.2

From the 1964 Mary Wells album
My Guy

MY GUY

Words and Music by
SMOKEY ROBINSON

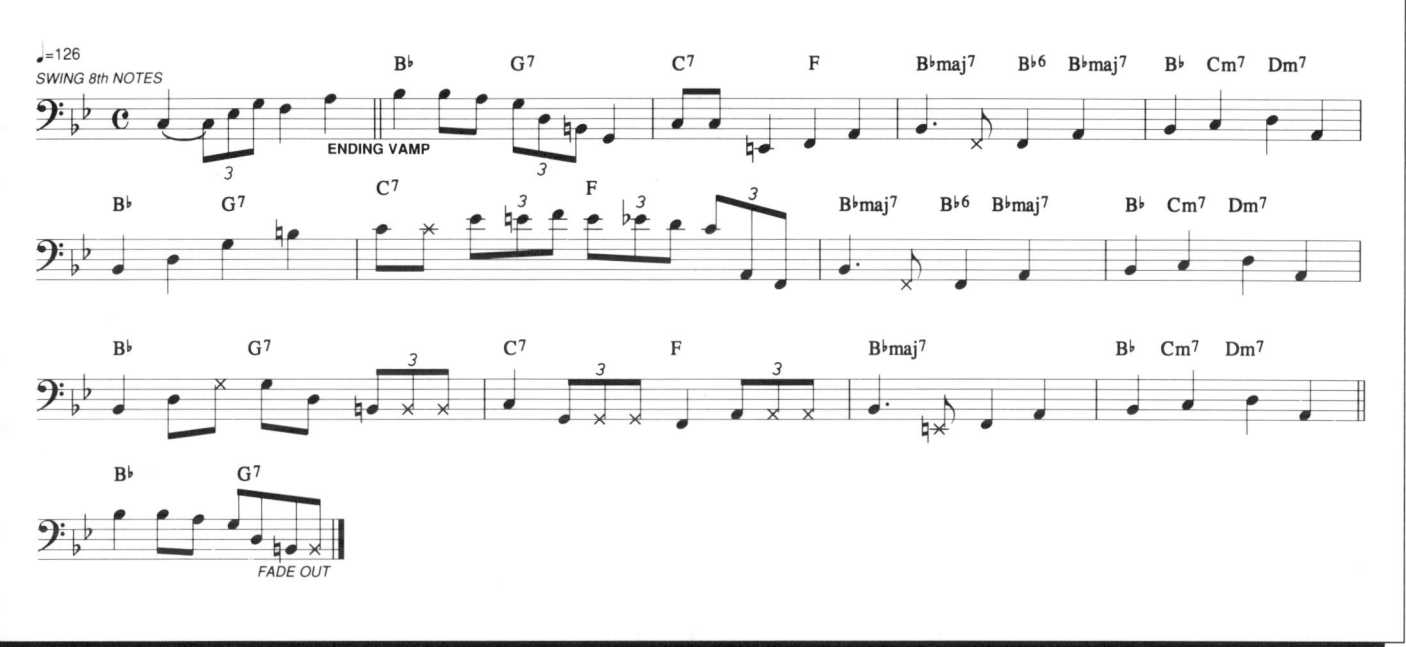

Standing in the Shadows of Motown

107

WILL LEE

When I requested a resume' from Will Lee's business office, I expected to be impressed with what they would send me, but I was totally unprepared for the ten page computer readout that accompanied his biography and photograph. Will has recorded with so many different artists that it took ten minutes just to read through the names starting with the letter "S." (And this list didn't even include his jingle and vocal sessions!)

With his ability to adapt to the different styles and demands of stars as diverse as Sinatra, James Brown, Scritti Politti, Earl Klugh, Bob Mintzer, Taj Mahal, George Benson, Michael Franks, Barry Manilow, Cher, the Miami Sound Machine, and Weather Report, it's no wonder that he has the unofficial title of "Busiest Bassist in New York." As if this isn't enough playing time for him, Will can also be found sitting in at clubs all over New York City with a variety of big bands and small Rock, Jazz, Pop, and Fusion ensembles.

However, most of you know him as the bass player who leaps out of your TV set at the beginning of every *Late Night with David Letterman* show. Being a member of "The World's Most Dangerous Band" is a perfect role for Will because of his stage presence, vocal ability, and his huge repertoire and overall knowledge of Pop, Rock, Blues, and R & B grooves from the last four decades. Check out his bass work some night and you may occasionally hear him performing the same version of "I Heard it Through the Grapevine" that he recorded for this project.

Musicians' Credits on Will Lee's Track

Keyboards: Paul Shaffer
Drums and Percussion: Will Lee
Arrangement transcribed by: Will Lee and Paul Shaffer
Recorded at Will Lee's home studio

I Heard It Through the Grapevine P.2

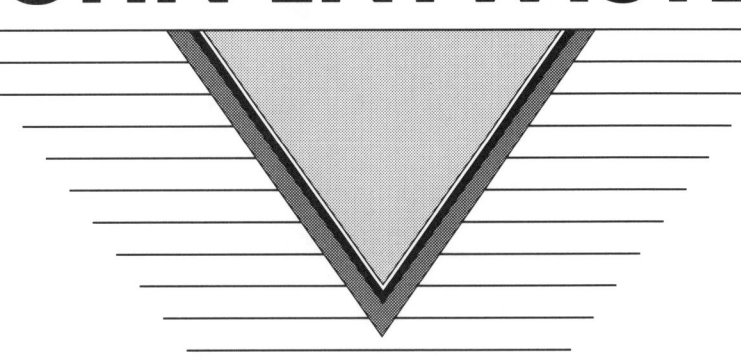

JOHN ENTWISTLE

Even though their styles are from two different worlds, I think that James Jamerson would have been really knocked out to know that a bassist of John Entwistle's stature wanted to be a part of his tribute. While James was pioneering his bass techniques in Detroit during the '60s, John was doing the same thing with his own style over in England. For more than twenty years, his thunderous bass lines have played a major role in the glorious history of the Who, and have strongly influenced electric bassists throughout the world.

Entwistle's bass playing on the live version of "My Generation" alone, put a lock on his place in the Rock and Roll Hall of Fame. Eighteen years after the release of the *Live at Leeds* album, many bassists are still trying to copy the style and tone of that electrifying performance.

John has also led a very successful solo career that has produced half a dozen albums and an excellent instructional tape and video (that's a part of Arlen Roth's "Hot Licks" catalogue). Even though the Who no longer tour, you can still get the opportunity to see John in person, because he's been playing the club circuits in Europe and the States with his own band.

If you happen to notice that John refers to Tamla instead of Motown in his introduction, that's because the sixties English releases of Motown hits were on the unified Tamla-Motown label, as opposed to the two separate labels that existed at the same time in the U.S.A.

Musicians' Credits on John Entwistle's Tracks

Guitars: Tina D. Blackman, Jeff Blackman, and Dr. Licks
Keyboards: Michael Rosenman
Drums: Keith Benson
Percussion: Mark Knox
Arrangements transcribed by: Dr. Licks
Engineered by Mark Knox at Strata

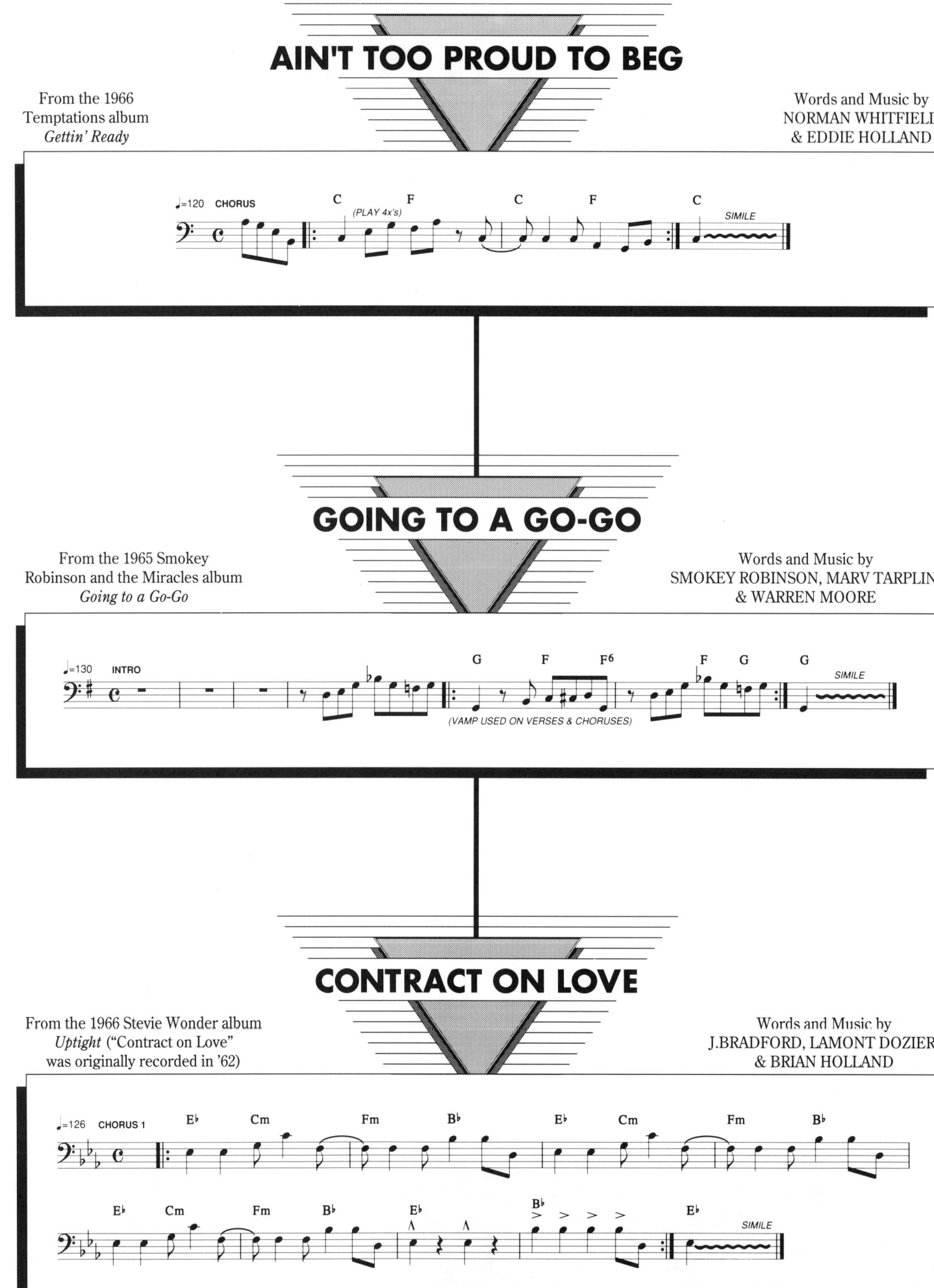

GERALD VEASLEY

There are very few bassists around who have led as eclectic a career as Gerald Veasley. Basically self taught and coming from a strong gospel influenced background, Gerald has spent the last ten years globe-hopping and recording with acts like Odean Pope, McCoy Tyner, jazz violinist, John Blake, Grover Washington Jr., Pat Martino, and the Dixie Hummingbirds. It doesn't make much of a difference to him whether he's performing with a straight ahead Jazz, Bebop, Avant-Garde, Rock, Funk, or Fusion artist. Gerald just wants to play.

In 1988, his years of dedication and hard work paid off when Joe Zawinul hired him to play with his newly evolved "Zawinul Syndicate." Gerald's solid groove and highly improvisational style was exactly what Zawinul was looking for. Jazz lovers must have felt the same way because Gerald's playing received rave reviews throughout The United States and Europe during the band's initial summer tour. In addition, he was voted to the number one spot in the *DOWNBEAT* Critics' Awards for "Talent Deserving Wider Recognition."

Gerald also holds a very important position in the evolution of this book; besides his dazzling performance on his teenage nemesis, "Darling Dear," Gerald Veasley is the musician who turned this author onto the bass artistry of James Jamerson.

Musicians' Credits on Gerald Veasley's Tracks

Keyboards: Fred Wackenhut
Guitars: Dr. Licks
Drums: Keith Benson
Percussion: Marc Knox and Johnny "O"
Arrangements transcribed by: Dr. Licks
Engineered by Marc Knox at Strata

Standing in the Shadows of Motown

113

Darling Dear P.2

SHOTGUN

From the 1965
Jr. Walker and the All Stars album
Shotgun

Words and Music by
AUTRY
DeWALT Jr.

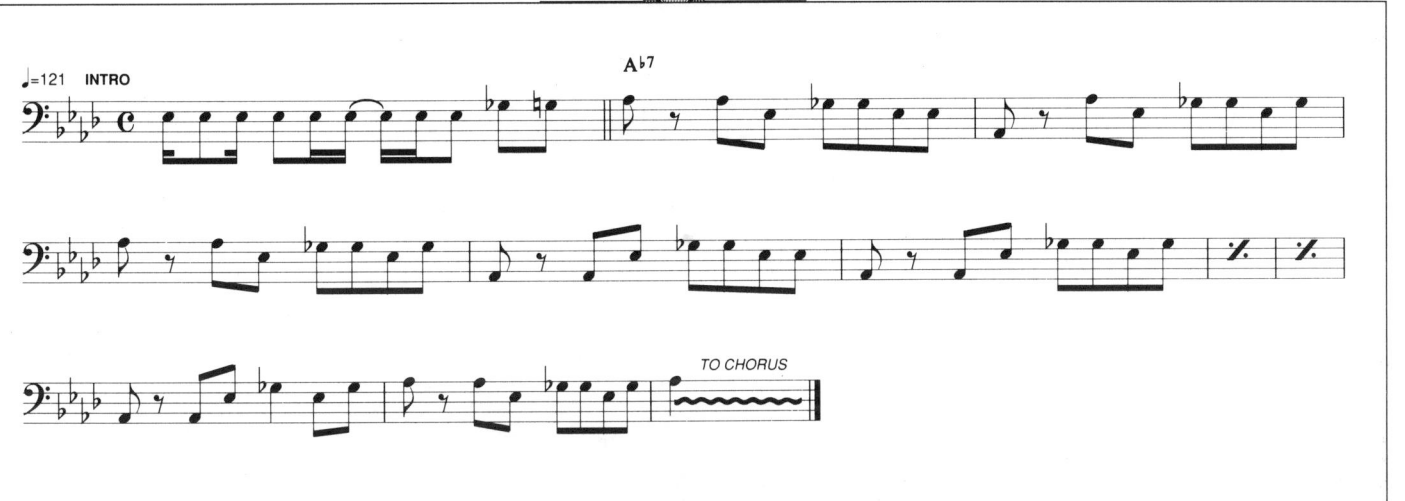

PHIL CHEN

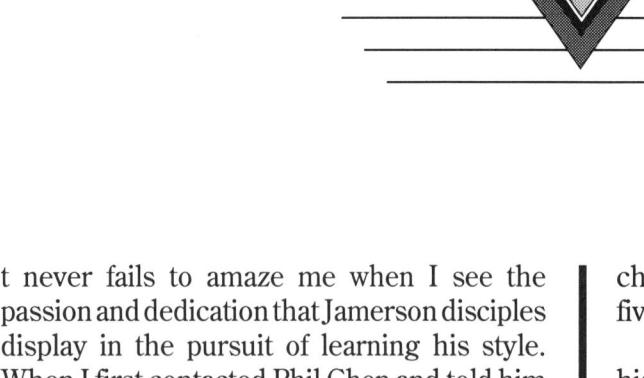

It never fails to amaze me when I see the passion and dedication that Jamerson disciples display in the pursuit of learning his style. When I first contacted Phil Chen and told him that I had transcribed over one hundred pages of Jamerson's bass lines, the first words out of his mouth were, "In measure 33 of 'I Was Made to Love Her,' was that third note a C natural or a C sharp?" When you walk into Phil's home studio, you enter "Jamersonville." Besides having pictures of James all over the place, he also has one of his Fender Precisions set up exactly like "the Funk Machine," and it's usually in close proximity to one of Phil's five or six Ampeg B-15's.

All this might cause you to think that Phil has spent his entire musical career chasing the ghost of James Jamerson, but nothing could be further from the truth. After leaving his hometown of Kingston, Jamaica at the age of 17, he began to pursue a very successful career as one of Rock and Roll's most sought after sidemen. Phil's reputation was earned during a five year stint as the bassist with Rod Stewart during the late '70s and early '80s, but the highpoint of his career came when he played on the Rock-Fusion classic, *Blow by Blow*, with Jeff Beck.

Since then, he has kept himself busy performing and recording with Eddie Van Halen, Brian May, Bob Marley, B.B. King, Bob Dylan, Dave Edmunds, Dion, Jimmy Cliff, Pete Townshend, the Eurhythmics, David Lindley, Jerry Lee Lewis, Little Richard, Jackson Browne, Keith Richards, and Eric Clapton (from the *Tommy* soundtrack).

Musicians' Credits on Phil Chen's Tracks

Keyboards: Tyrone "Jumpie" Downie
Drums and Percussion: Alvino Bennett
Knee Slaps: Alvino Bennett and Steve Brown
Guitars: Dr. Licks
Arrangements transcribed by: Lou Shoch and Dr. Licks
Engineered by Phil Kenzie at Kenzie studios

PINO PALLADINO

James Jamerson's bass lines traveled a great distance from Detroit. In fact, they traveled far enough to inspire a promising young Welsh bassist named Pino Palladino, to move to London and pursue a recording career that would ultimately lead to dates with stars like Elton John, Tears For Fears, David Gilmour, Chaka Khan, Pete Townshend, Joan Armatrading, The Edge, and Gary Numan. In recent years, his brilliant work with Paul Young has given him international recognition as one of the world's premier fretless electric bassists.

Pino is a master craftsman when it comes to tone and all the subtle nuances that his bass has to offer. While the rich dull thud of James Jamerson's bass sound is worlds removed from the very alive eighties sound that he evoked on Paul Young's "Every Time You Go Away," Pino had no trouble at all when it came to matching Jamerson's '60s sound for his performance on the tape that accompanies this book.

It was pretty obvious that Pino had an all time favorite Jamerson track because when I sent him a large selection of some of James' greatest lines, without hesitation, he asked if anyone had chosen "For Once In My Life." His re-creation of this track had a much better start than the original. He cranked it out in about one week. The original Motown track inexplicably sat on a shelf in Detroit for two years before being released. I think it was well worth the wait—don't you?

Musicians' Credits on Pino Palladino's Tracks

Guitars: Steve Boltz
Keyboards: Richard Dunn
Drum machine programming: Pino Palladino
Arrangements transcribed by: Richard Dunn, Steve Boltz, and Pino Palladino
Engineered by Dai Shell at Circus studios in London and The Music Factory in Cardiff

FOR ONCE IN MY LIFE

From the 1968 Stevie Wonder album *For Once in My Life*

Words and Music by ORLANDO MURDEN & R. MILLER

For Once in My Life P.2

I SECOND THAT EMOTION

From the 1968 Smokey Robinson & the Miracles album *Greatest Hits Vol. 2* (recorded in '67)

Words and Music by SMOKEY ROBINSON & AL CLEVELAND

(I KNOW) I'M LOSING YOU

From the 1967 Temptations album *With a Lot O' Soul*

Words and Music by NORMAN WHITFIELD, EDWARD HOLLAND, & CORNELIUS GRANT

GEDDY LEE

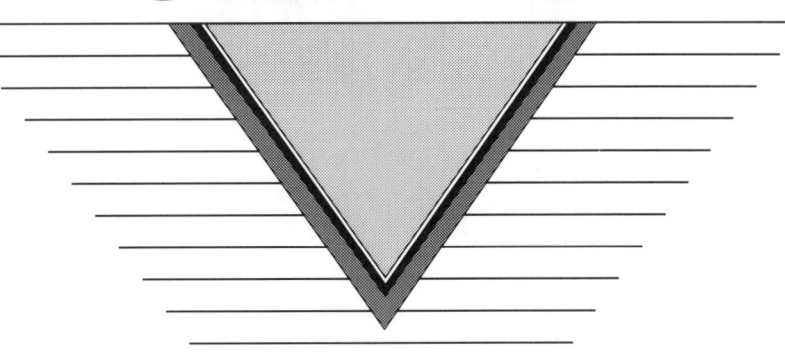

Extraordinary talent comes in many forms. Take James Jamerson, whose fat, low-end bass sound contributed to the success of hundreds of different acts during his career. At the extreme opposite end of the musical spectrum we have multi-instrumentalist, Geddy Lee, whose biting, high-end bass lines and creative synthesizer work have been heard for the last twenty years with just one band. But that band just happens to be one of the most innovative of all the supergroups of arena rock . . . Rush.

The one thing that they do have in common (aside from the brilliance of their bass playing) is the massive impact that each one of these artists has had on the bass world. Thousands of R&B players have tried to get the "Jamerson Sound," while their counterparts in the world of Rock and Roll have been running around buying up Steinberger and Rickenbacker basses in efforts to sound just like the bass parts on "Tom Sawyer" and "The Spirit of Radio."

Geddy has come a long way since Rush's 1968 bar band days when they played covers of Cream, Led Zeppelin, and Jeff Beck tunes. After a decade and a half of sold-out concerts all over the world (not to mention sixteen albums), Geddy shows no signs of slowing down. *GUITAR PLAYER* magazine recently relegated him to their "Gallery of the Greats" after realizing that they better give some other bassists a chance to win in the "Best Rock Bass" category of their reader's poll. Geddy won the award five years in a row.

Musicians' Credits on Geddy Lee's Track

Guitars: Dr. Licks
Drums: Sal Labruna
Percussion: Johnny "O"
Keyboards: Sal Labruna and Mark Knox
Arrangement transcribed by: Dr. Licks
Engineered by Mark Knox at Strata

GET READY

From the 1966 Temptations album
Gettin' Ready

Words and Music by
SMOKEY ROBINSON

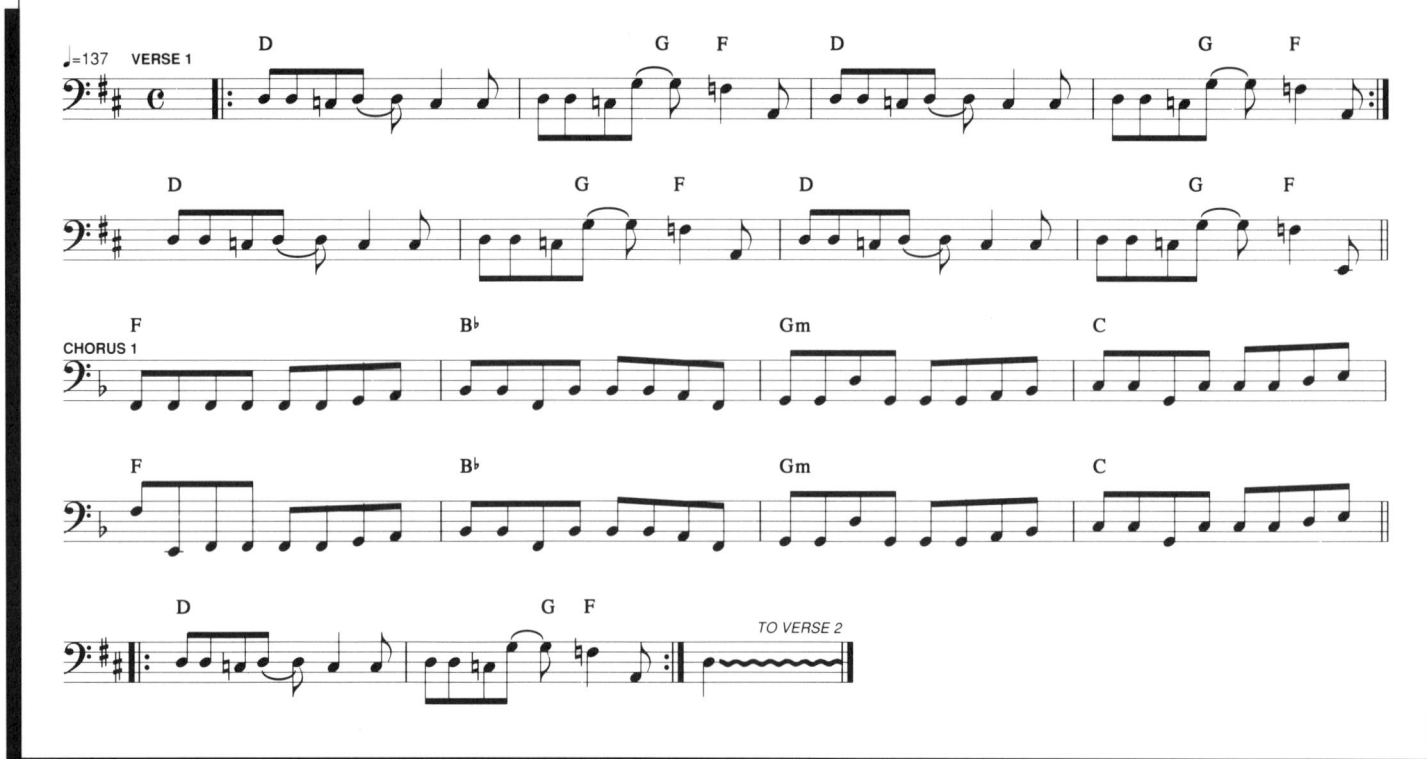

CHUCK RAINEY

If you ever discuss musical influences with almost any R&B, Jazz, or Pop electric bassist, the name Chuck Rainey will appear 99.99% of the time. In fact, prior to the new techniques and styles pioneered by Larry Graham and Jaco Pastorius, most R&B bass players usually admitted to being either James Jamerson or Chuck Rainey disciples.

His legendary sessions and tours with stars like Quincy Jones, Aretha Franklin, Donald Byrd, Steely Dan, Harry Belafonte, Sam Cooke, the Crusaders, and King Curtis' All Stars (during the 1965 Beatles tour) have earned him an important place in music history. For the past two decades, Chuck has also been a fixture at Montreaux, Newport, Cannes, and other music festivals, backing up Jazz and Blues musicians like Gato Barbieri, Freddie Hubbard, Paul Butterfield, and Stanley Turrentine. If you think you can escape his sound by turning off your stereo or radio, think again, because every time you tune in to a *M*A*S*H* rerun, or a late night film like *Midnight Cowboy*, or *Three Days of the Condor*, listen closely and you'll hear his unmistakable bass.

Not one to rest upon past laurels, Chuck's never ending quest for musical innovation, along with his country roots, have led him to pursue a career as a solo artist. He describes his new one man show concept as "Funky Folk Music." If you're lucky enough to catch his act, you'll hear him sing, tell jokes and stories, and play some of the most creative bass lines that ever came out of a Fender Precision.

Musicians' Credits on Chuck Rainey's Tracks

Keyboards: Lou Cianciulli and Mark Knox
Drums: Alzonia Johnson and Keith Benson
Guitars: Ron Jennings, Jeff Blackman, Tina D. Blackman, and Dr. Licks
Percussion: Bob Farina
Arrangements transcribed by: Dr. Licks
Engineered by Dennis Nardi and Mark Knox at Strata

BERNADETTE

From the 1967 Four Tops album *Reach Out*

Words and music by
HOLLAND—DOZIER—HOLLAND

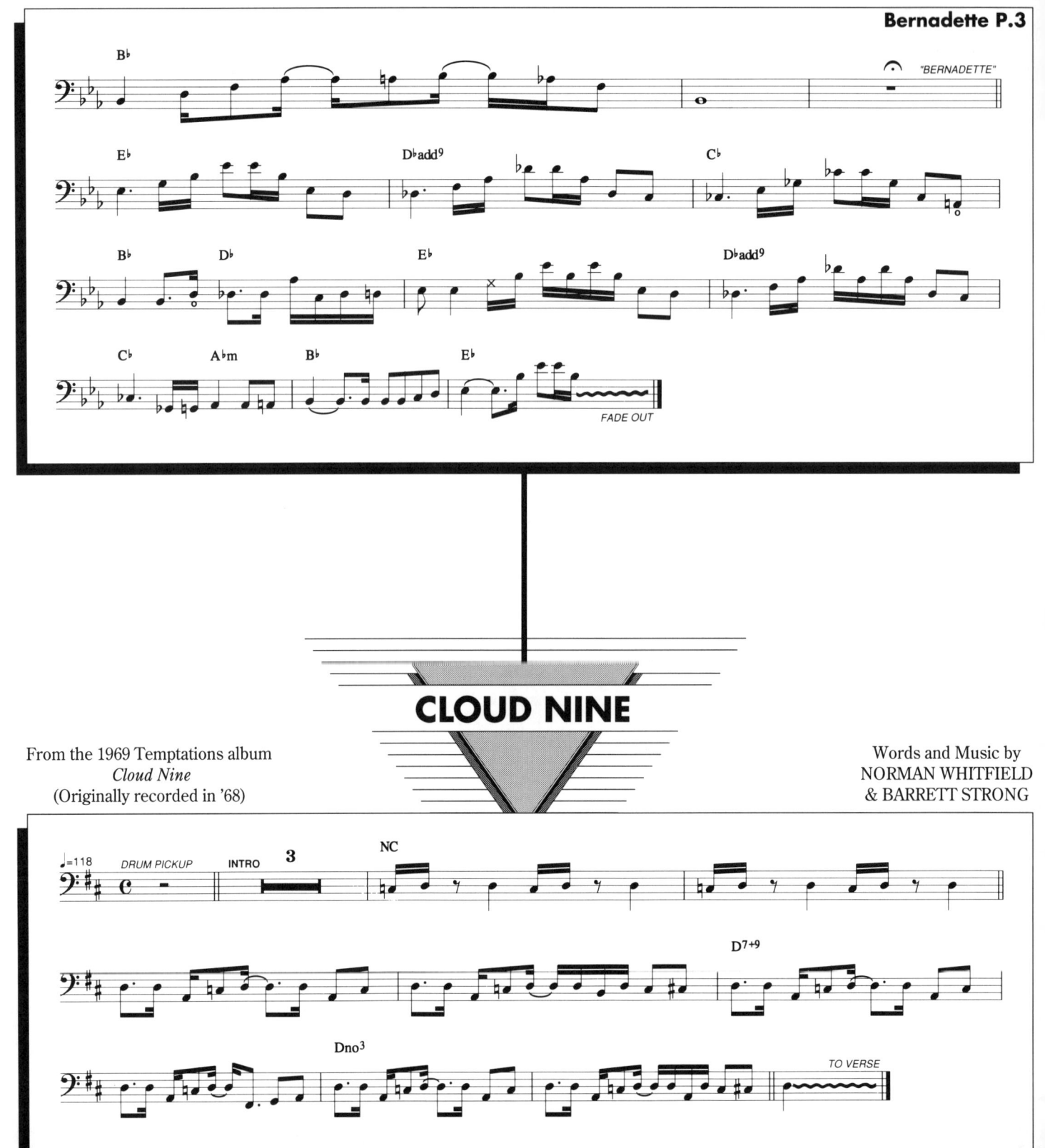

CLOUD NINE

From the 1969 Temptations album
Cloud Nine
(Originally recorded in '68)

Words and Music by
NORMAN WHITFIELD
& BARRETT STRONG

YOU KEEP ME HANGING ON

From the 1967 Supremes album
The Supremes Sing Holland—Dozier—Holland
(Originally recorded in 1966)

Words and Music by
HOLLAND—DOZIER—HOLLAND

THE PHILADELPHIA INTL.
RHYTHM SECTION

Very few musicians can lay claim to being part of the house band for a major R&B label—but Jimmy Williams and Keith Benson can. Jimmy's bass playing and Keith's drumming can be heard on hundreds of cuts released by Philadelphia International Records. Just like James Jamerson, Jimmy and Keith are "behind the scenes" musicians. Very few people outside of Philly have heard of them, yet their recording sessions with acts like the O'Jays, Patti Labelle, the Four Tops, Grace Jones, Curtis Mayfield, Charo, the Stylistics, the Intruders, Lou Rawls, Robert Palmer, Teddy Pendergrass, and Edgar Winter have resulted in over 30 gold and platinum records.

You say that you still don't know who they are? Well, do you remember the great bass line hook on McFadden and Whitehead's quintuple platinum smash, "Ain't No Stoppin' Us Now?" That was Jimmy. Or how about the serious pocket on Robert Palmer's "Every Kinda' People?" Keith is very proud of what his drumming did for that track.

Even though they both come from a rival R&B label, their love and admiration for the work of Jamerson, the Funk Brothers, and Motown in general, became apparent to me when I worked with them on "Ain't No Mountain High Enough." Aside from the reverence with which they approached the project, it was difficult to shut them up during playbacks because they were too busy doing their Marvin Gaye and Diana Ross imitations—vocal inflections and all.

Musicians' Credits on the Philadelphia Intl. Rhythm Section's Tracks

Guitars: Dr. Licks
Keyboards: Fred Wackenhut
Drums and percussion: Keith Benson
Arrangements transcribed by: Dr. Licks
Engineered by Mark Knox at Strata

Ain't No Mountain High Enough P.2

AIN'T NO MOUNTAIN HIGH ENOUGH

From the 1970 Diana Ross album *Diana Ross*

Words and Music by VALERIE SIMPSON & NICKOLAS ASHFORD

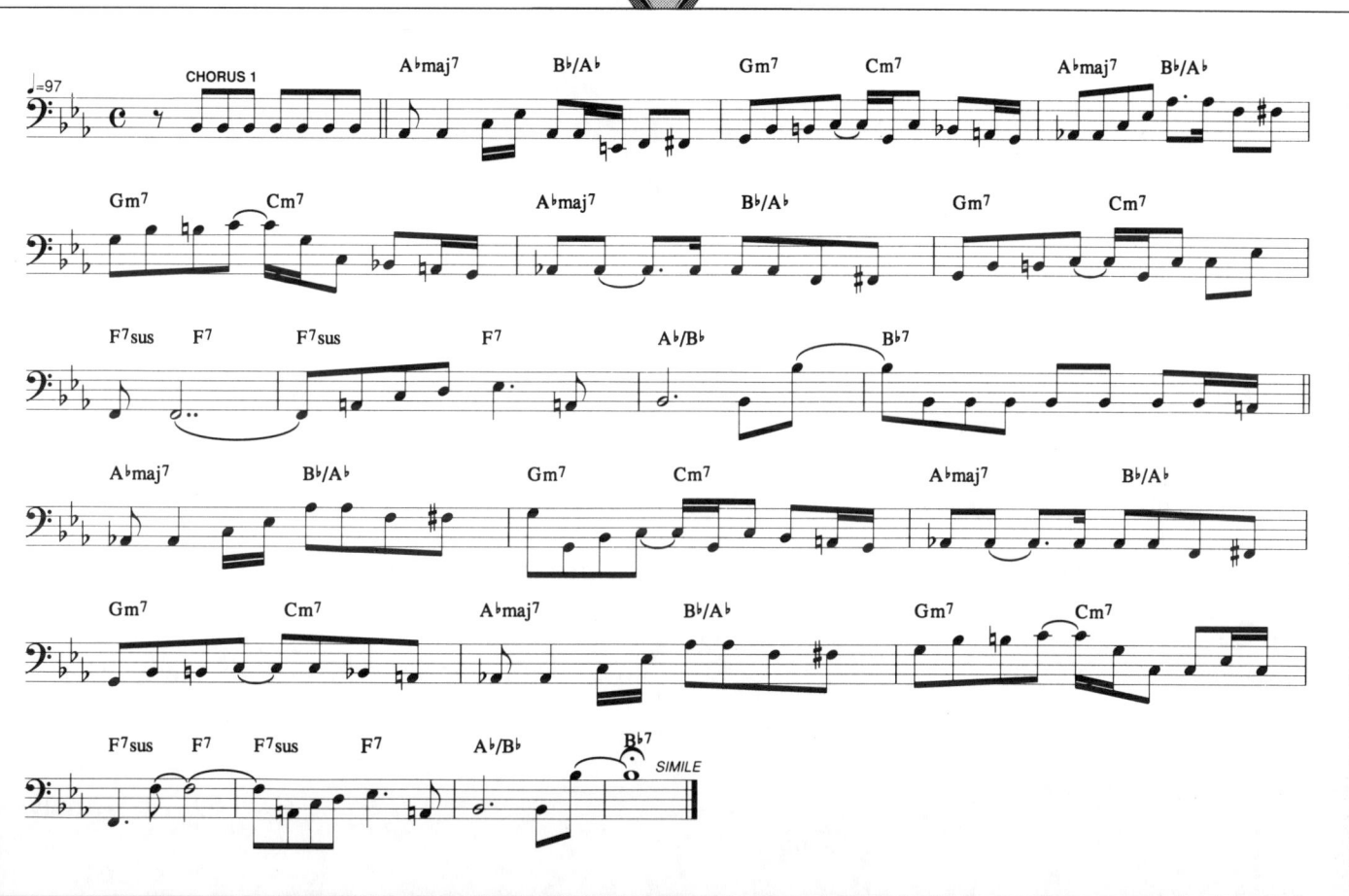

Ain't No Mountain High Enough-Modulated Bridge

READY FREDDY WASHINGTON

T he music coordinators and contractors who put together the *Motown 25* show had their pick of the world's finest bassists; their selection was "Ready" Freddy Washington. This wasn't a choice governed by connections, politics, or any of the usual avenues of employment in the entertainment industry. Freddy's studio and concert track record earned him the right to play the show.

It also wasn't just a coincidence that The National Association of Recording Arts and Sciences made him a nominee for the award of "Best Studio Bassist of 1987." Freddy's touring and recording work with artists like Jeffrey Osbourne, DeBarge, Patrice Rushen, Al Jarreau, Kenny Rodgers, and Herbie Hancock has been nothing short of brilliant. His bass playing also helped Dionne Warwick, Stevie Wonder, Gladys Knight, and Elton John win a Grammy for their 1987 recording of "That's What Friends Are For."

My experience with Freddy during the recording session for "I'm Gonna Make You Love Me" made me aware of the level of expertise that is necessary to become a top echelon studio bassist. You may have noticed that the bass chart for "I'm Gonna' Make You Love Me" is fairly complex. (A gross understatement if there ever was one.) Well, Freddy sight read it down the first take! Even though we made a few more passes to clean up some things on the track, you might want to keep his performance in mind if you ever set your sights on getting involved in the New York or L.A. recording scenes.

Musicians' Credits on Ready Freddy's Tracks

Keyboards: Buca Pecuna
Drum machine programming: Mark Knox
Guitars: Dr. Licks
Arrangements transcribed by: Dr. Licks
Engineered by Mark Knox at Strata

I'M GONNA MAKE YOU LOVE ME

From the 1968 album
*Diana Ross and the Supremes
Join the Temptations*

Words and Music by
KENNY GAMBLE, JERRY ROSS,
& JERRY WILLIAMS

I'm Gonna Make You Love Me P.2

GIRL (WHY YOU WANNA MAKE ME BLUE)

From the 1965 album
The Temptin' Temptations
(Recorded in '64)

Words and Music by
NORMAN WHITFIELD
& EDDIE HOLLAND

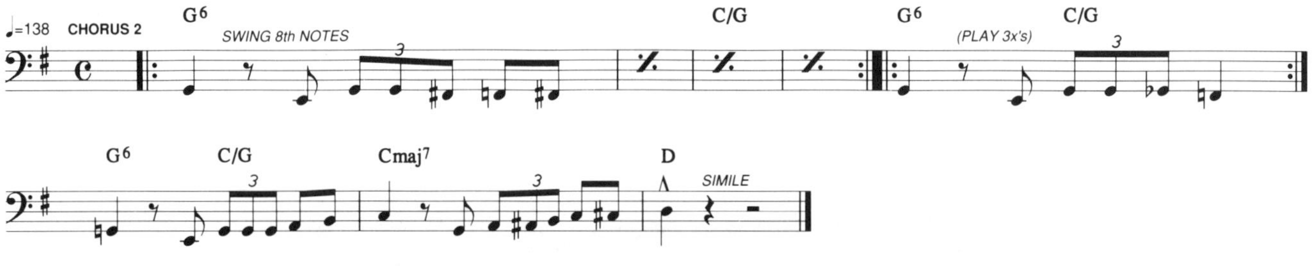

GARRY TALLENT

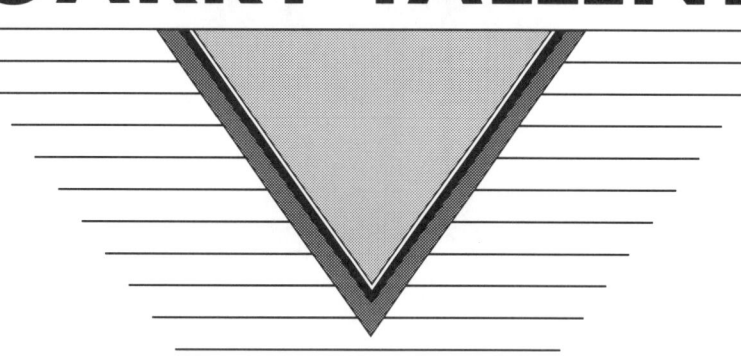

In an industry that is inundated with overblown egos and self-absorbed displays of technical prowess, a musician like Garry Tallent is a breath of fresh air. Gary's approach to playing the bass has always been focused on contributing to the overall feel and groove of a song, as opposed to getting in as many hot licks as possible within a three and a half minute format. If the success of the tune requires Garry to play quarter notes, or whole notes, or even no notes at all, that's what he'll do.

In Garry's case, nice guys don't always finish last. His unselfish attitude was rewarded with one of the most important positions in all of Pop music—the role of bassist for Bruce Springsteen. Like his boss, Garry was an important part of the New Jersey Rock and Roll club scene in the '60s. After years of studying the styles of some of his musical heroes like Hank Williams, Buddy Holly, and Rolling Stones bassist, Bill Wyman, Garry became involved with a band called the Moment of Truth—one of the hottest acts playing the Jersey shore in 1968.

Joining the E Street Band three years later in 1971, he began to evolve into an integral part of Bruce Springsteen's overall sound. In his customary understated style, Garry comments, "What I do-nobody notices 'til it stops." For the sake of millions of music fans around the world, let's all hope that it doesn't stop anytime soon.

Musicians' Credits on Garry Tallent's Track

Keyboards: Jim Bannach
Footstomps and tambourine: Phil Taormina, Jeff Blackman, and Dr. Licks
Drums: Keith Benson
Guitar: Dr. Licks
Arrangement transcribed by: Dr. Licks
Engineered by Jim Bannach at BLT studios

BABY LOVE

From the 1965 album
Where Did Our Love Go?
(Recorded in '64)

Words and Music by
HOLLAND—DOZIER—HOLLAND

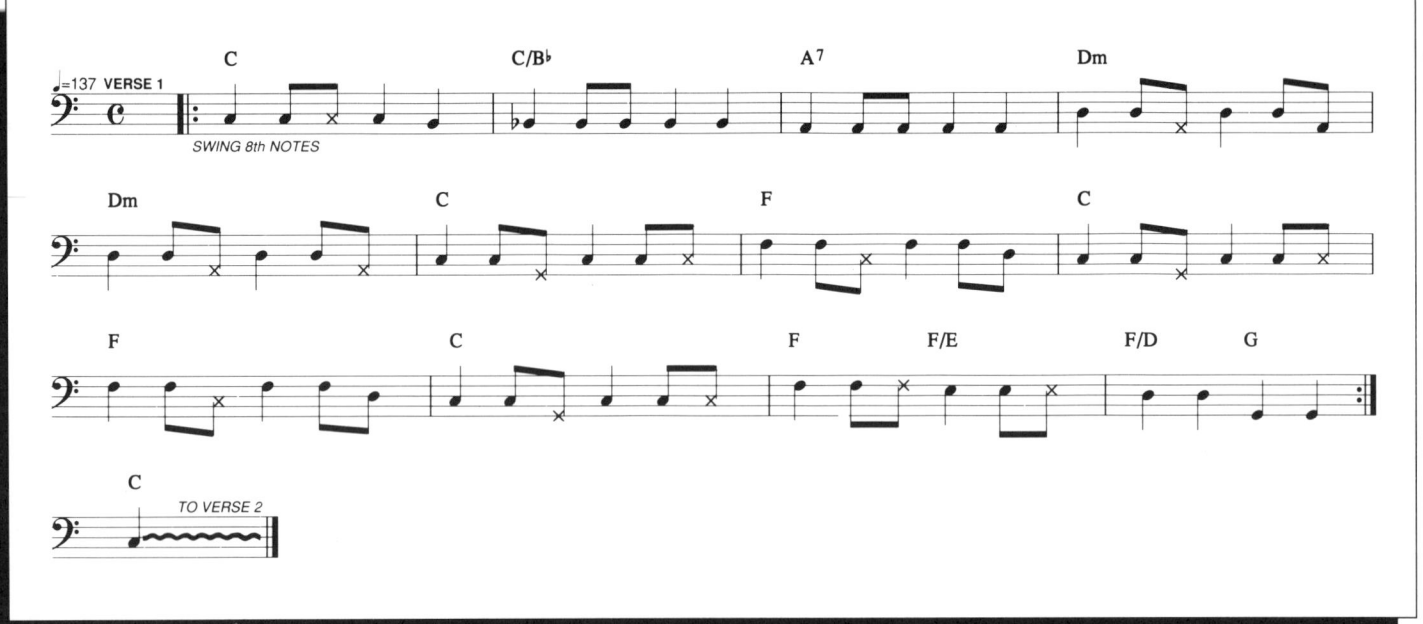

ALLEN McGRIER

When James Jamerson Jr. asked me to include his friend Allen McGrier in the guest artists section of this book, he told me that, "Dad would have wanted him in the book because they were good friends." So I figured, "Well, who am I to argue with James Jamerson Sr?" But, after receiving his rendition of "It's a Shame" and reading through his recording credits, I realized that there was much more to this selection than just politics and family ties.

There is a certain attitude and approach to playing Detroit music that can be learned, but it's probably much easier if you happened to grow up in the midst of the scene like Allen did. In addition to having the advantage of living in Detroit in the '60s and '70s, he also spent some of his teenage years hanging out at one of the shrines of the Motown groove . . . James Jamerson's house!

Allen is mostly known for his work as a bassist, songwriter, arranger, and producer with R&B vocal star, Teena Marie, but he has also had extensive recording and touring experience with the Dells, Ray Parker Jr., Rick James and the Stone City Band, the Jones Girls, Cheryl Lynn, the Mary Jane Girls, and the New Edition. As of this writing, his most recent composition for Teena Marie entitled "Ooh-La-La-La," is climbing the charts and heading for Gold.

Musicians' Credits on Allen McGrier's Track

Keyboards: George Akerley
Drums: Joe Nero
Percussion: Bob Conga
Guitars: Josh Sklair
Arrangement transcribed by: Dr. Licks
Engineered by Allen McGrier at his home studio and mixed by Dennis Nardi at Strata

IT'S A SHAME

From the 1970 Spinners album *Second Time Around*

Words and Music by STEVIE WONDER, SYREETA WRIGHT, & LEE GARRETT

JOHN PATITUCCI

John Patitucci occupies a special place not only in this book, but in the contemporary music scene. Like James Jamerson, who he acknowledges as one of his primary influences, John is one of the few bassists around who is a virtuoso on both upright and electric bass. In fact, the National Association of Recording Arts and Sciences thought enough of his upright playing to offer him the 1986 NARAS MVP award for acoustic bass.

But it's his phenomenal prowess on the six string electric bass that has earned him international recognition. He may credit bassists like Jamerson, Willie Weeks, Steve Swallow, Stanley Clarke, Jaco Pastorius, and Larry Graham as being his most important teachers, but he owes just as much to saxophone players like Michael Brecker and Sonny Rollins for the fluid, legato style horn lines that flow from his instrument.

John has been developing his style in the West Coast music scene since 1979, playing with jazz and fusion greats like Wayne Shorter, John Scofield, Stan Getz, Freddie Hubbard, Tom Scott, Lee Ritenour, Dave Grusin, Larry Carlton, and Clare Fischer. His big break came in 1985 when he got the chance to flex his chops as a member of the Chick Corea Elektric Band. However, there's a lot more to this multi-talented musician than just extraordinary technique. In 1988, after recording two Elektric Band albums with Chick, John got the chance to show off his own compositional skills on his debut solo album for GRP records entitled, *John Patitucci*.

Musicians' Credits on John Patitucci's Tracks

Guitars: Dr. Licks
Keyboards: Lou Cianciulli
Drums: Carl Mottola and Ted Greenberg
Percussion: Carl Mottola and Mark Knox
Arrangements transcribed by: Dr. Licks
Engineered by Bob Rust at Strata

HOW SWEET IT IS (TO BE LOVED BY YOU)

From the 1966
Jr. Walker and the All Stars album
Road Runner

Words and Music by
HOLLAND—DOZIER—HOLLAND

HEAT WAVE

From the 1963 Martha and the Vandellas album *Heat Wave*

Words and Music by HOLLAND—DOZIER—HOLLAND

MICKEY'S MONKEY

From the 1963 Miracles album *Doin' Mickey's Monkey*

Words and Music by HOLLAND—DOZIER—HOLLAND

JIMMY HASLIP

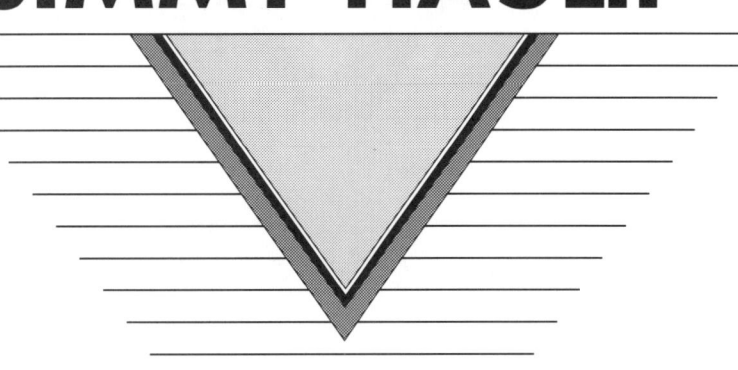

I had to get at least one lefty in here just to prove that Jamerson's lines work from both sides of the fingerboard. I don't think that I could have found anyone better than Jimmy Haslip. He's not just lefthanded; he also plays upside down like another "Jimi" that we all know about. Nevertheless, whether he plays upside down or inside out, his sound and concept have made him one of the recording industries most sought after session players.

As a studio bassist, Haslip's credits look like the combined R&B, Rock, and Jazz racks at a Sam Goody record store. On the surface, it would seem that he is cut from the hired gun mold because of all the freelance recording and touring that he's done with stars like Chaka Kahn, Ron Wood, David Sanborn, Al Jarreau, Donald Fagen, Rod Stewart, Bruce Hornsby, and Crosby, Stills, and Nash. However, his true musical passion involves more of a teamwork concept.

Together with the rest of his buddies in his own group, the Yellowjackets, Jimmy was nominated for a Grammy Award for their 1983 album entitled, *Mirage a Trois*. Following the release of their *Shades* album three years later, "the Jackets" eventually scored a Grammy for "Best Rhythm and Blues Instrumental." (You can also hear some of their compositions and performances on the soundtrack for *Star Trek IV*.)

Musicians' Credits on Jimmy Haslips's Tracks

Synclavier programming:
Steve Croes
Arrangements transcribed by:
Jimmy Haslip and Steve Croes

DON'T MESS WITH BILL

From the 1966 Marvelettes album *Greatest Hits*

Words and Music by SMOKEY ROBINSON

Don't Mess With Bill P.2

IT'S THE SAME OLD SONG

From the 1965 Four Tops album
Second Album

Words and Music by
HOLLAND—DOZIER—HOLLAND

SHAKE ME, WAKE ME (WHEN IT'S OVER)

From the 1966 Four Tops album
On Top

Words and Music by
HOLLAND—DOZIER—HOLLAND

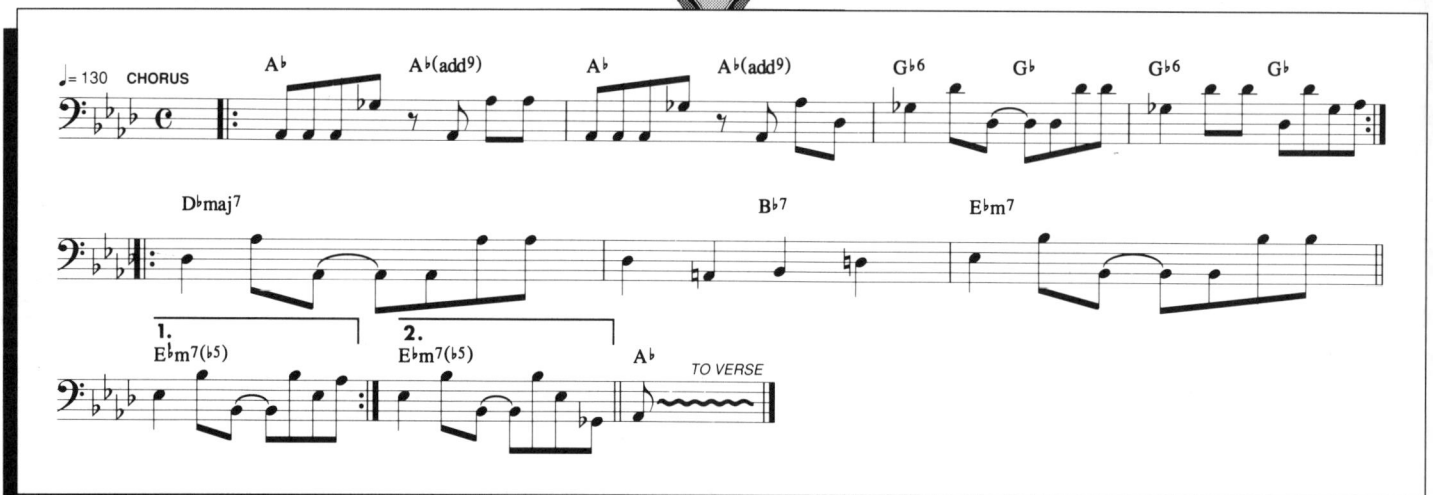

BOB BABBITT

In 1925, Wally Pipp had the unenviable position of being the second string first baseman for the New York Yankees. Why was this such a bleak situation? Because the first string first baseman was Lou Gehrig and there was no way that Wally would ever get to play.

At first glance, it would seem that Bob Babbitt was in the same predicament because in the late '60s, he was hired by Motown to play some bass. The only problem was that James Jamerson was the first string bassist (no pun intended). But unlike poor old Wally, Bob did get to play some bass—some great bass. Just listen to what he did on Marvin Gaye's "Inner City Blues," or Smokey Robinson and the Miracles' "Tears of a Clown," or the Temptations' "Ball of Confusion" and you can see that he earned the right to play on those historic sessions.

Bob's career didn't end after Motown's departure from Detroit. He quickly relocated into the New York and Philadelphia recording scenes and began racking up dates on almost 200 top 40 hits with artists like Elton John, the Stylistics, Bette Midler, Jeff Beck, Meatloaf, Jimi Hendrix, the Spinners, Chuck Berry, and Englebert Humperdink. Bob currently resides in Nashville where he continues to pursue his recording career. But at this point in his life, he can relax; he has nothing to prove. His place in Pop music history has long been secured because, after all, he *was* the man who "gave you some bass with those 88's" on the Capitol's, "Cool Jerk."

Musicians' Credits on Bob Babbitt's Tracks

Drums: Keith Benson
Percussion: Mark Knox
Guitars: Ron Jennings and Dr. Licks
Keyboards: Buca Pecuna and Mark Knox
Horns: Evan Solot, Ron Kerber, and Bill Zaccagni
Arrangements transcribed by: Dr. Licks
Engineered by Mark Knox at Strata

AIN'T NOTHING LIKE THE REAL THING

From the 1968 Marvin Gaye-Tammi Terrell album *You're All I Need*

Words and Music by VALERIE SIMPSON & NICKOLAS ASHFORD

Ain't Nothing Like the Real Thing P.2

UPTIGHT (EVERYTHING'S ALRIGHT)

From the 1966 Stevie Wonder album *Uptight*

Words and Music by STEVIE WONDER, HANK COSBY, & SYLVIA MOY

(I'M A) ROAD RUNNER

From the 1966 Jr. Walker and the All Stars album *Road Runner*

Words and Music by HOLLAND—DOZIER—HOLLAND

WILLIE WEEKS

One of the most frustrating of the many music industry pitfalls that successful studio players must face is typecasting. Everyone loves to put labels on musicians: "this guy is an R&B player;" "this guy is only a jazz player;" or "this guy is a heavy metal headbanger;" and so on. Willie Weeks had the good sense to just ignore it all and concentrate on making good music. With touring and recording credits like the Rolling Stones, Joe Walsh, Aretha Franklin, Elton John, George Harrison, the Doobie Brothers, and James Taylor, you can see that his talents enabled him to cross over into any field in which he felt like playing.

Willie has been on the scene making great music since 1966, but he feels that his finest work came in the early and mid '70s with the late Donny Hathaway. His bass solo on "Everything is Everything" off of the *Donny Hathaway Live* album is a classic example of his playing style during this period. As Willie explains, "I used to pattern myself after James Jamerson and Ray Brown, but as I got older and my musical tastes began to mature, I tried to fit into the groove of whatever artist I was working with. By the time I was with Donny, I had my own style."

After twenty years of touring and recording, Willie has settled down to a slightly quieter existence in Tennessee, but he still continues to play and record in and around Nashville.

Musicians' Credits on Willie Weeks' Tracks

Guitars: Dr. Licks
Percussion: Mark Knox
Keyboards: Marcie Rauer and Sal Labruna
Drum machine programming: Willie Weeks
Keyboards: Sal Labruna and Mark Knox
Arrangements transcribed by: Dr. Licks
Engineered by Dennis Nardi at Strata

STILL WATER (LOVE)

From the 1970 Four Tops album *Still Waters Run Deep*

Words and Music by SMOKEY ROBINSON & FRANK WILSON

MY BABY LOVES ME

From the 1966 Martha and the Vandellas album *Greatest Hits*

Words and Music by WM. STEVENSON, SYLVIA MOY, & IVY HUNTER

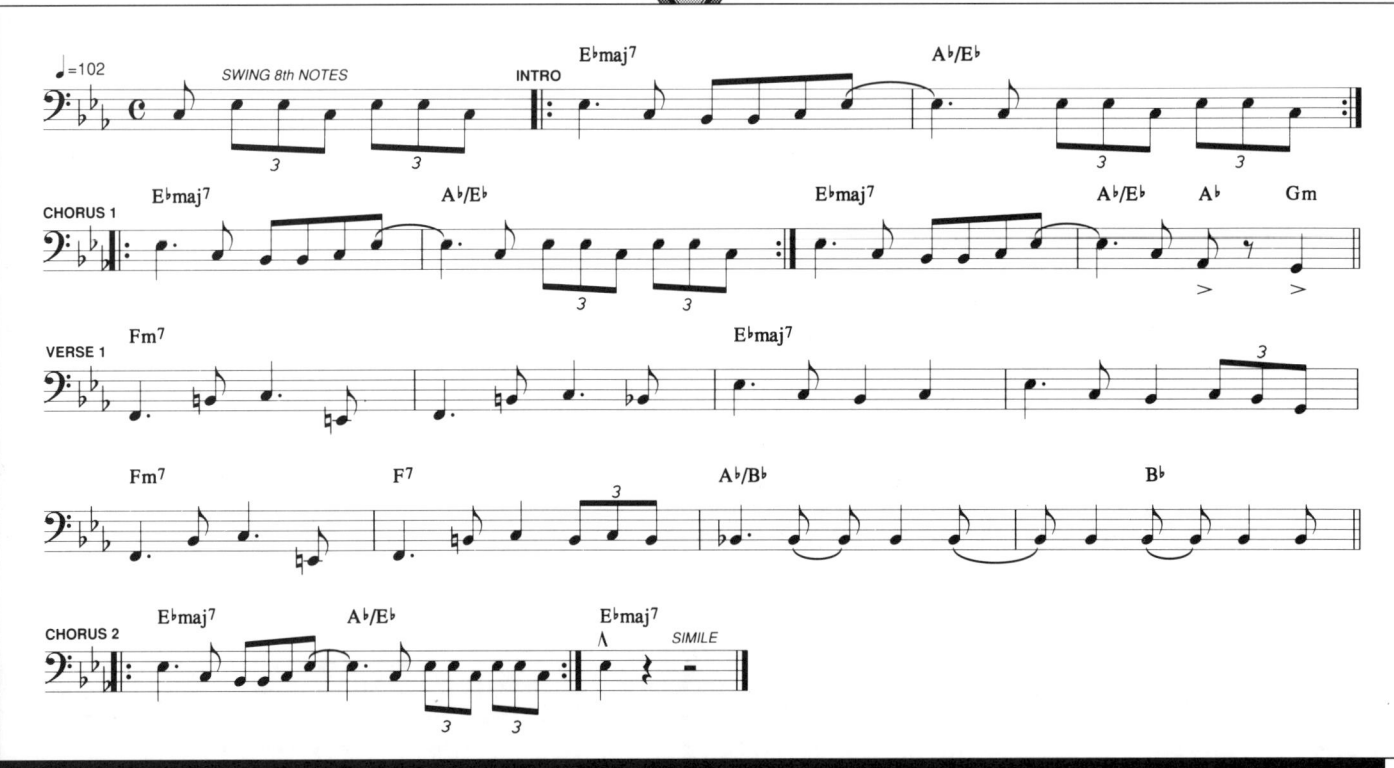

DAVE HUNGATE

ost people know David Hungate as being one of the founding members of the Grammy award winning group, Toto. Four successful albums (including the smash hit, "Rosanna") have allowed him the professional freedom to do anything he wants. And that's just what David did; he packed his bags and moved to Nashville where he is very involved in session work and a solo album soon to be released on Impression records.

However, Nashville was not the first studio scene of which David was a part. After attending North Texas State University where he was a member of the NTSU lab band that performed at the 1970 Montreux Jazz Festival, David migrated to the West Coast and became one of L.A.'s most in demand session bassists. Check the recording credits on some of the albums by Boz Scaggs, Diana Ross, Alice Cooper, Kiki Dee, Sarah Vaughn, or Olivia Newton-John and you're likely to see his name in print.

In the mid '70s, David was occasionally booked as a standby on a few of the West Coast sessions that were supposed to be played by James Jamerson. As David related to me, "James was such a genius that producers were willing to pay an extra bassist to be on call just in case he didn't show up, or if he had an off day. I can't think of too many musicians who they would do that for, but it was well worth the money because when he was on top of it, *nobody* was better."

**Musicians' Credits on
David Hungate's Track**

Keyboards: Lou Cianciulli
Guitars and drum machine programming: David Hungate
Arrangement transcribed by: Dr. Licks
Engineered by David Hungate at his home studio

HOME COOKIN'

From the 1969 Jr. Walker and the All Stars album *Home Cookin'*

Words and Music by
MELVIN MOY, HANK COSBY
& EDDIE WILLIS

Home Cookin' P.2

FRANCIS ROCCO PRESTIA

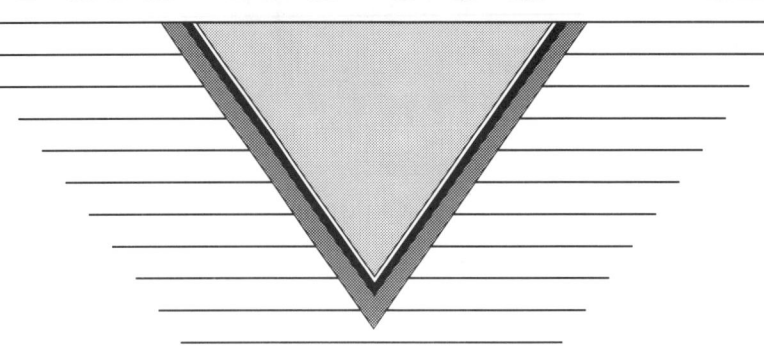

The hardest working right hand in the bass business has to belong to Francis "Rocco" Prestia. There has been a steady stream of staccato 16th notes and offbeat accents flowing out of the West Coast ever since he exploded on the Pop music scene as a member of the Rolls Royce of Funk bands, Tower of Power.

If you've ever tried to play any of Rocco's bass parts, you have my sympathy. Your hands are probably just starting to uncramp. The technical demands of playing his lines from Tower of Power songs like "Soul Vaccination," "You've Got to Funkifize," or "What is Hip" are overshadowed only by the creativity and originality of his melodic ideas and overall concept.

When Rocco handed in his tape of "Just a Little Misunderstanding," he told me that he never realized how deeply James Jamerson had affected his playing until he had to sit down and actually play one of his bass parts note-for-note. But the similarities in these two bassists run much deeper than just notes or rhythms. Both Jamerson and Rocco are the originators of unique schools of bass playing that have been copied all over the world. Everyone from Jeff Berlin to Nathan East credits Rocco as having been a major influence on their playing style. But just as there was only one James Jamerson, there is only one Francis Rocco Prestia. There isn't a bassist alive who sounds like either of them.

Musicians' Credits on Rocco Prestia's Track

Drums: Bob Farina
Keyboards: Marc Luperini
Guitars: Dr. Licks
Arrangement transcribed by: Dr. Licks
Engineered by Mark Knox at Strata

JUST A LITTLE MISUNDERSTANDING

From the 1966 Contours single
Just a Little Misunderstanding
(never released on an album)

Words and Music by
LUVEL BROADNAX, STEVIE WONDER,
& CLARENCE PAUL

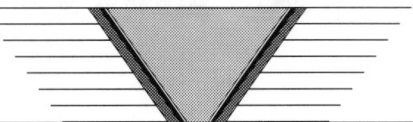

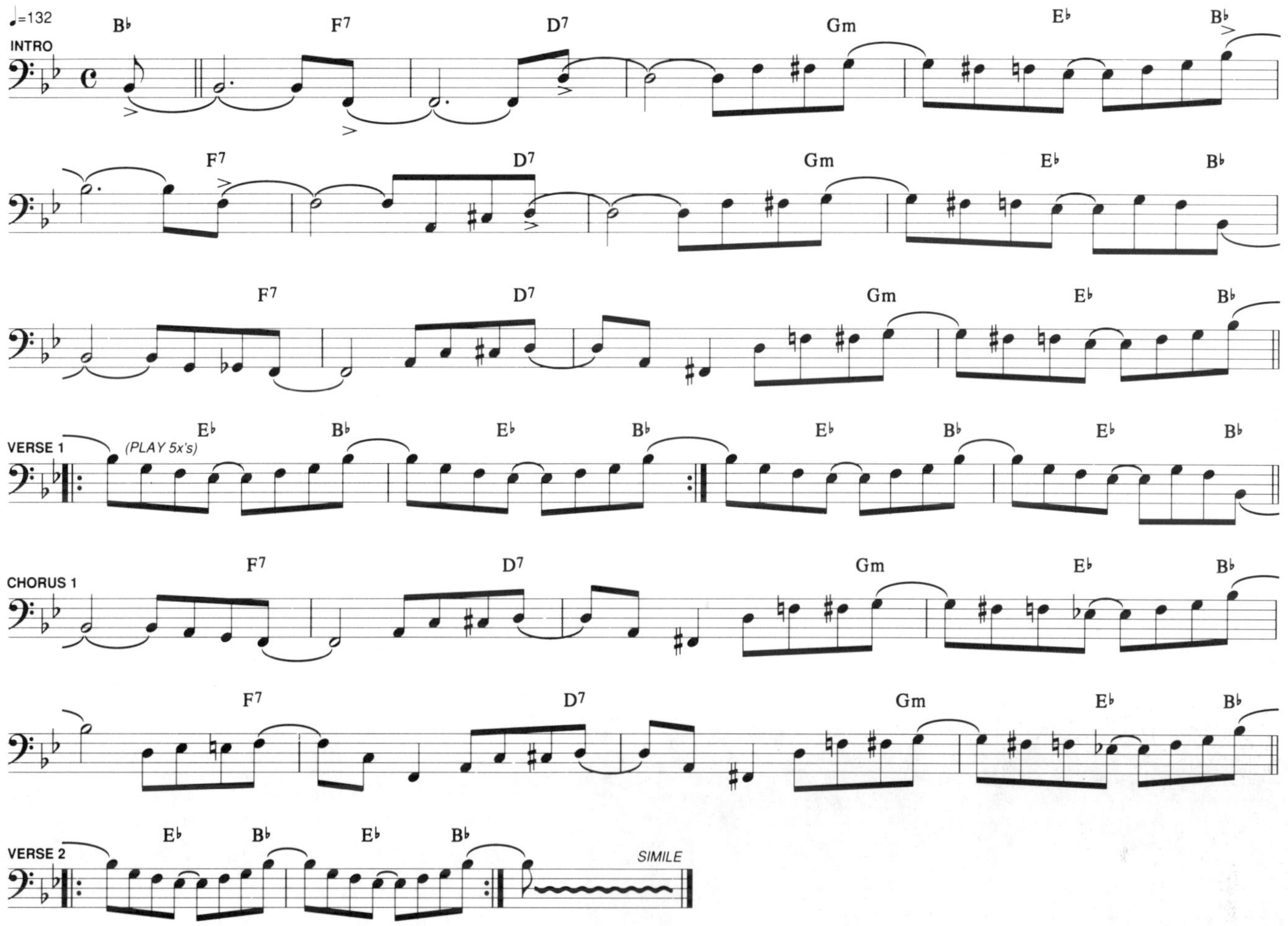

JACK BRUCE

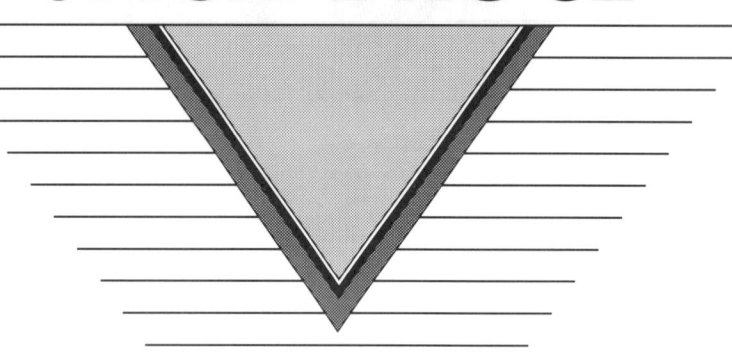

If there is a counterpart to James Jamerson in the world of Rock and Roll, it would have to be Jack Bruce. Just as James brought R&B and Pop bass playing out of the Dark Ages, Jack was primarily responsible for the renaissance of Rock bass. Furthermore, both Jamerson and Bruce started out playing acoustic Jazz bass and eventually wound up trying to push a highly melodic electric bass style on a music scene that was accustomed to bassists playing mostly roots and fifths. From that point on, their paths diverged as Jamerson settled into a career as a studio musician and Jack pursued live performance and recording work with his own groups.

After playing in the mid-sixties with Graham Bond and Manfred Mann, Jack's revolutionary bass concept came of age when he joined Cream in 1966. This move helped to usher in "The Age of the Rock and Roll Musician as Virtuoso." The extended improvisations and experiments in volume, distortion, and feedback that Cream became known for helped to make them the yardstick against which all subsequent power trios would be compared.

But Jack Bruce's career was far from over when he parted company with Eric Clapton and Ginger Baker in 1968. Making full use of his vast musical background, Jack has continued to freely cross back and forth between the Rock and Jazz worlds, recording albums and touring throughout the '70s and '80s with acts like West, Bruce, and Laing, Tony Williams' Lifetime, Robin Trower, Larry Coryell, Carla Bley, and his own group, Jack Bruce and Friends.

Musicians' Credits on Jack Bruce's Track

Keyboards: George Akerley
Drums and Percussion: Alzonia Johnson
Guitars: Lou Maresca and Dr. Licks
Arrangement transcribed by: Dr. Licks
Engineered by Bob Rust at Strata

COME 'ROUND HERE (I'M THE ONE YOU NEED)

From the 1966 Smokey Robinson and the Miracles album *Away We A Go-Go*

Words and Music by HOLLAND—DOZIER—HOLLAND

Standing in the Shadows of Motown

163

KENNY AARONSON

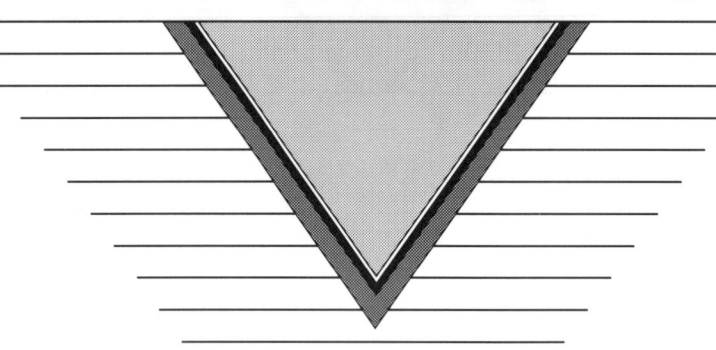

Longevity has always been a rare commodity amongst Rock and Roll and Pop musicians. In an industry where new performers tend to rise and fall within a few short years, veterans like Kenny Aaronson are a special breed. Remember way back in 1973, a band called Stories had a #1 platinum smash titled "Brother Louie"? Kenny was in that group. But instead of fading out like so many others, he spent the next fifteen years touring and recording with artists like Billy Idol, Bob Dylan, Foghat, Billy Squier, Brian Setzer, Hall & Oates, Rick Derringer, Sammy Hagar, and Dave Edmunds. He has also played on filmscores like *Porky's Revenge,* and appeared on the *MTV* special *Guitar Greats*.

What has helped to maintain Aaronson's status as one of Rock and Roll's busiest sidemen? Kenny attributes much of his success to a mid-career realization that he had to become more fluent in some of the Blues, R&B, Country, and Rockabilly styles that are the roots of Pop music. His efforts to round out his musical background led him to an in depth study of '50s and '60s bass styles, and in particular, the techniques of his favorite player, James Jamerson. Kenny must have learned his Motown lessons well, because he walked into his Jamerson session with a big chunk of foam stuffed under the bridge of his Precision bass.

If you happen to think that studying older styles of music like Motown, Rockabilly, and Memphis is a waste of time, think again—and follow Kenny's example. He was just voted "Best Bassist of 1988" in the most recent *ROLLING STONE* critics poll.

Musicians' Credits on Kenny Aaronson's Tracks

Keyboards: Joshua Yudkin
Drums: Carl Mottola
Percussion: Jeff Feinberg
Guitars: Dr. Licks
Baritone Sax: Michael Pedicin Jr. and Bill Zaccagni
Arrangements transcribed by: Dr. Licks
Engineered by Bob Rust at Strata

LOVE IS LIKE AN ITCHING IN MY HEART

From the 1966 Supremes album
The Supremes A Go-Go

Words and Music by
HOLLAND—DOZIER—HOLLAND

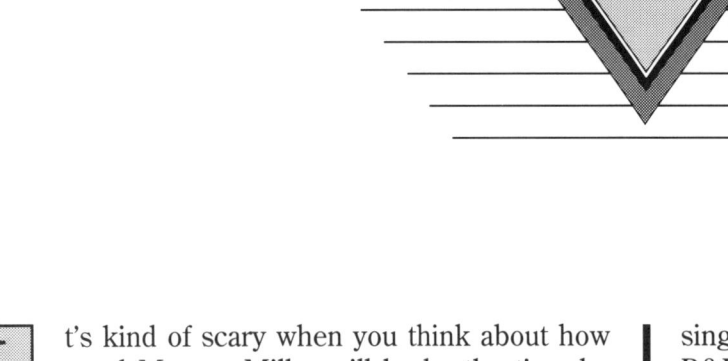

MARCUS MILLER

It's kind of scary when you think about how good Marcus Miller will be by the time he turns 30. Still in his mid-twenties, he has already won a Grammy, recorded two solo albums, and produced or played on a string of highly successful records with Luther Vandross, David Sanborn, Elton John, Miles Davis, Roberta Flack, Lonnie Liston Smith, Bob James, Paul Simon, and dozens of other artists. As if that isn't enough, Marcus has also written songs for vocal stars like Teddy Pendergrass, Dionne Warwick, and Aretha Franklin.

The origins of his musical career are a bit more humble. Marcus moved to Queens in 1973 and started singing with neighborhood groups, basically mimicking R&B hits by the Jackson Five and the Sylvers. At the age of 13, he decided that he wanted to be a bass player and over the next few years would add clarinet, saxophone, keyboards, guitar, and drums to his growing repertoire. By the late '70s, Marcus had worked himself into the New York Jazz and studio scenes, beginning a busy apprenticeship in the recording world.

Once his big break came in 1981, he was well prepared. As a member of the *Saturday Night Live* band, Marcus became friendly with saxophonist David Sanborn and eventually collaborated with him on the critically acclaimed *Voyeur* album. Their close relationship continues to this day, as Marcus is presently the music director and bassist for Sanborn's syndicated cable TV show, *Sunday Night*.

Musicians' Credits on Marcus Miller's Track

Drums: Keith Benson
Percussion: Dr. Licks
Guitars: Dr. Licks
Keyboards: Ted Baker
Arrangement transcribed by: Dr. Licks
Engineered by Bob Rust at Strata

I Was Made to Love Her P.2

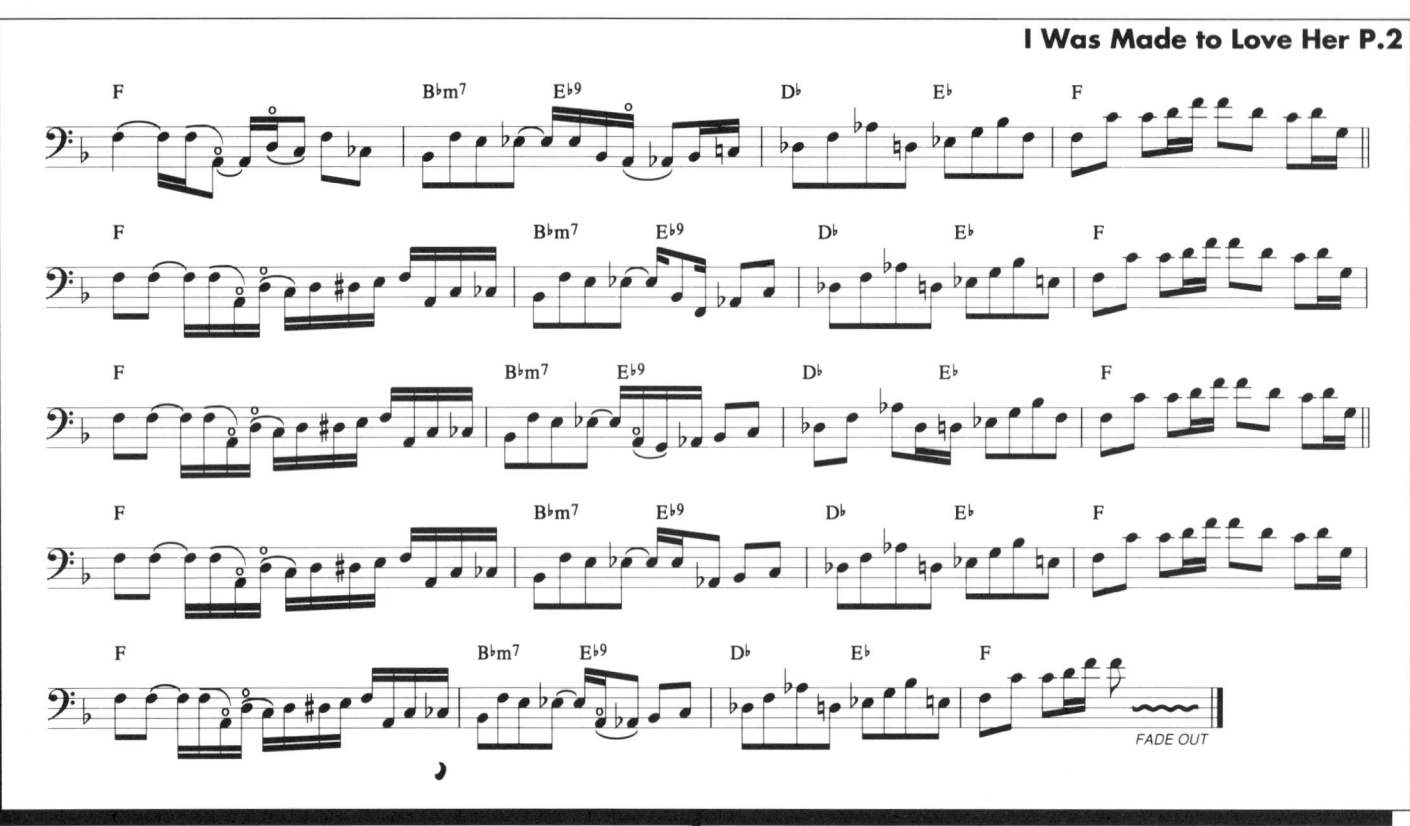

NATHAN WATTS

On a cold Detroit winter afternoon in 1962, a wide-eyed, eight year old Nathan Watts peeked into the basement window of Hitsville's studio in hopes of catching a glimpse of one of the hometown stars. Never in his wildest dreams could he have imagined that he would eventually become a part of the rich musical history that flowed from that building. Even more amazing was the fact that after playing bass for *only* two years, he was hired by Stevie Wonder.

Fourteen years, five continents, and thousands of concerts later, Nathan is still right in the middle of all of Stevie's grooves.

Even though "Nate" occupies one of the most coveted sideman positions in R&B, he has never been content to restrict his creativity to just working for Stevie. His bass playing has also provided solid bottom on hits by Paul McCartney ("Say, Say, Say"), Lionel Ritchie, the Pointer Sisters, Diana Ross ("Muscles"), Sergio Mendes, Seals and Crofts, Jeffrey Osbourne, the Jacksons, and hundreds of other R&B and Pop acts.

Although he was self taught, Nate credits Detroit's bass scene as being his primary influence. James Jamerson, Bob Babbitt, Michael Henderson, and Tony Newton all had a hand in shaping his style, but Nate's simple, down-to-earth approach towards bass playing is all his own. "When I play, I'm just trying to make people feel good and enjoy themselves. Whatever it takes to do that, that's what I'll play." Judging by the smiles on peoples' faces at Stevie Wonder concerts, I guess Nate must be doing his job.

Musicians' Credits on Nate Watts' Track

Guitars: Dr. Licks
Keyboards: Lou Cianciulli
Drums and Percussion: Bob Farina
Arrangement transcribed by: Dr. Licks
Engineered by Bob Rust at Strata

NOWHERE TO RUN

From the 1965 Martha and the Vandellas album *Dance Party*

Words and Music by HOLLAND—DOZIER—HOLLAND

Nowhere to Run P.2

NON-MOTOWN MEDLEY

The documentary tapes that accompany this book would not be complete without including some of the bass work that James Jamerson did outside of Motown. While his West Coast studio career never reached the artistic heights of his Detroit period, he still made significant contributions on many of the dates on which he played. Here are a few of the more successful (and recognizable) recordings that James was involved with:

1) **"Your Love Keeps Lifting Me (Higher And Higher)" by Jackie Wilson**
Words and Music by C. Smith, G. Jackson, and R. Miner
Bass part played by Steve Bescrone

2) **"Rock The Boat" by the Hues Corporation**
Words and Music by W. Holmes
Bass part played by Jimmy Hoff

3) **"Boom Boom" by John Lee Hooker**
Words and Music by John Lee Hooker
Upright bass part played by Craig Thomas

4) **"Boogie Fever" by the Sylvers**
Words and Music by K. St. Lewis and Freddie Perren
Bass part played by Phil Taormina

5) **"Which Of Us Is The Fool" by Robert Palmer**
Words and Music by Robert Palmer
Bass part played by Reggie Hamilton

6) **"You Don't Have To Be A Star (To Be In My Show)" by Marilyn McCoo & Billy Davis Jr.**
Words and Music by J. Dean and J. Glover
Bass part played by Larry "G" Goldman

Musicians' Credits for the Non-Motown Medley
Trumpet: Rick Kerber
Tenor Sax: Ron Kerber
Keyboards: Mick Rossi
Guitars: Dr. Licks and Larry "G" Goldman
Drums percussion and drum machine programming: Bob Farina
All arrangements by Dr. Licks
Recorded at Audio Plus, Strata, and Gee Whiz studios

BASIL FEARRINGTON

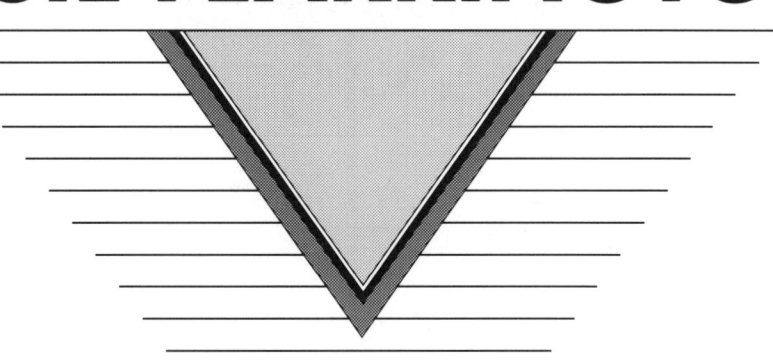

The "Unsung Bass Hero" role is not the sole property of James Jamerson. The R&B and Pop music scenes have created quite a few musicians who can lay claim to that title. For instance, take the strange case of Basil Fearrington. His name may not be on the tip of every music lovers tongue, but his sound certainly is. Unless you've been living on a deserted South Pacific island for the past decade or so, you've definitely heard his artistry behind acts like Peabo Bryson, David Spinozza, Phyllis Hyman, Lou Rawls, Sister Sledge and Teddy Pendergrass. In the midst of all these R&B and Pop sessions, Basil also managed to squeeze in some time to tour and record with Jazz-Fusion violinist, Michal Urbaniak.

However, some of Basil's finest work came into focus during a seven year association with Roberta Flack that resulted in three albums and the smash hit, "The Closer I Get to You." This proved to be a real stepping stone for him because Roberta's rhythm section eventually became the house band for Mtume'/Lucas Productions where they racked up three platinum albums behind Stephanie Mills (including the Grammy award winning "Never Knew Love Like This Before").

Basil claims that his best music teacher has been his massive 2500 album record collection. Being an admitted "Jamerson addict," you can guess which LP's have the deepest wear marks.

Musicians' Credits on Basil Fearrington's Tracks

Keyboards: Lou Cianciulli
Knee Slaps and Guitars: Dr. Licks
Drum machine programming: Mark Knox and Dr. Licks
Arrangements transcribed by: Dr. Licks
Engineered by Dennis Nardi and Mark Knox at Strata

LOVE IS HERE AND NOW YOU'RE GONE

From the 1967 Supremes album
The Supremes Sing Holland—Dozier—Holland

Words and Music by
HOLLAND—DOZIER—HOLLAND

SINCE I LOST MY BABY

From the 1965 Temptations album *The Temptin' Temptations*

Words and Music by SMOKEY ROBINSON & WARREN MOORE

Standing in the Shadows of Motown

I'M WONDERING

Basil Fearrington

From the Stevie Wonder Anthology
Looking Back
(Originally recorded in '67)

Words and Music by
STEVIE WONDER, SYLVIA MOY,
& HANK COSBY

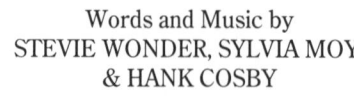

ANTHONY JACKSON

nthony Jackson once stated in a *GUITAR PLAYER* interview, "Everything I am as a musician is because of James Jamerson." Because of this, I'm sure you can understand why he was the first of the guest artists that I contacted when I decided to write this book. Anthony has been spreading the gospel about Jamerson long before I even knew who Jamerson was. His devotion to his childhood idol almost borders on the religious.

However, there is much more to Anthony Jackson than just his role as the keeper of James Jamerson's flame. Throughout his career, Anthony has pursued a level of artistic integrity and uncompromised musical excellence that has been an inspiration to bassists all over the world. From Quincy Jones film scores like "The Wiz," to the Funk of Chaka Kahn, to the Jazz stylings of pianists Michel Camilo and Chick Corea, the recording industry has sought his expertise in almost every form of music known to man.

Anthony's longevity in the forefront of the bass world belies his relatively young age. Almost two decades ago when he was still in his teens, he cut one of the most original and influential bass lines in the history of Rhythm and Blues—the phasored, plectrum, mega-funk part on the O'Jays' "For the Love of Money."

For the past fifteen years, Anthony has been pioneering both the instrumental construction and stylistic development of the six string bass, or as he refers to it, "the contrabass guitar." Unless the music world loses it's groove or it's sanity, you'll probably be hearing Anthony's low B string rumbling around on recordings for years to come.

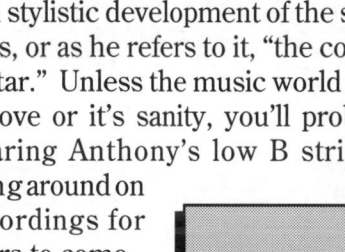

**Musicians' Credits on
Anthony Jackson's Track**

Keyboards: Gary Haase and Anthony Jackson
Percussion: Anthony Jackson
Drums: Casey Conrad
Guitars: Ron Jennings and Dr. Licks
Arrangement transcribed by: Anthony Jackson and Dr. Licks
Engineered by Anthony Jackson at his home studio

HOW LONG HAS THAT EVENING TRAIN BEEN GONE

From the 1968
Diana Ross and the Supremes album
Love Child

Words and Music by
FRANK WILSON &
PAM SAWYER

Performance Notes

1) Notes with ✱ are barely audible.

2) Notes connected with a bracket are to be plucked in one motion with a right hand "rake."

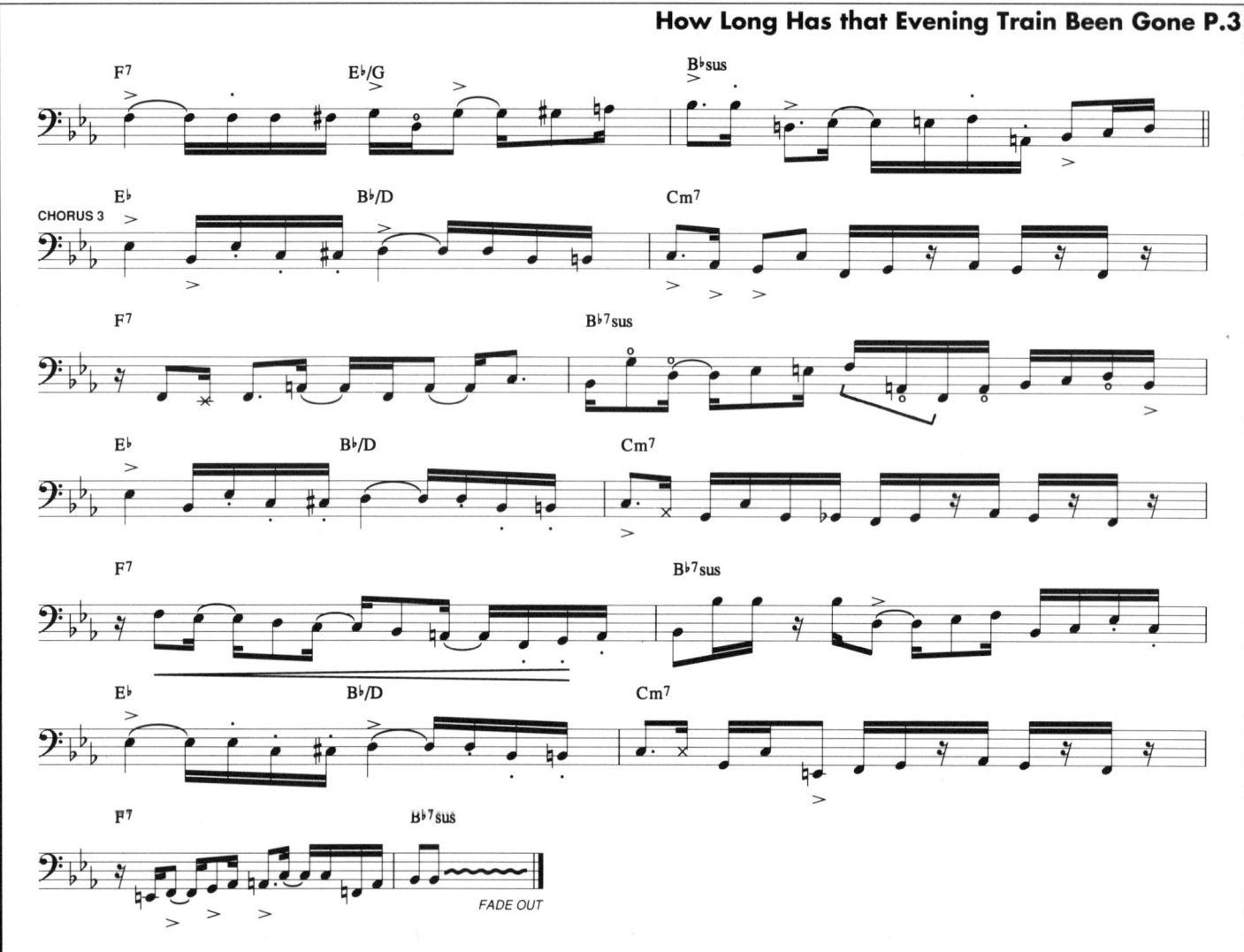
How Long Has that Evening Train Been Gone P.3

KUDOS

> "There was only one Jamerson. All the rest were imitators—just like there was only one Charlie Parker. You ever heard of Phil Woods and Cannonball Adderley? They're great but they are not Charlie Parker. They're just imitators. There was only one Charlie Parker and there was only one James Jamerson."
>
> —GIL ASKEY—
> Motown arranger and conductor

> "I was playing in a background horn section at this club in Detroit and Jamerson came in, not knowing the material. After we ran the tune down once, he was reading the music and after that, he put the music away and never looked at it again. He had an uncanny knack of putting everything in it's proper place so that it gave the whole band support. He was nothing short of amazing. He changed his sound around to accommodate the tune; he didn't make the tune fit him. He put the other musicians in the band at ease and probably made us play a bit over our heads because he gave us such support with his selflessness."
>
> —GROVER WASHINGTON JR.—
> Saxophonist

> "When Jamerson recorded, he'd blow everybody's mind. They'd sit back and wait on Jamerson. He always came up with something unique and dynamite. He never played you the same lick twice. They'd give him some chordsheets and they'd say, 'Give me something James.'"
>
> —MARTHA REEVES—
> Motown recording artist

> "James Jamerson was the epitome. He started Fender bassing. All that funk bassing—Jamerson was it. He started all that bottom thing, and even though Motown had a pop sound, they still had some serious bass in that shit. Like Stevie's record [sings] 'I was born in Little Rock...' Man, the track to that would kick ass."[6]
>
> —GEORGE CLINTON—
> Founder of Parliament-Funkadelic, and master of extra-terrestrial funk

> "I played for years with Jamerson and then I played with other bass players, but it's hard for me to enjoy my gig as much anymore because I was spoiled for life."
>
> —URIEL JONES—
> Motown drummer

> "I was one of his biggest fans. I spent time studying his bass lines before I even knew him. 'For Once in My Life' is phenomenal. That's a concerto for bass. He used to do things that sounded like he was going lower than the E, and I thought that he tuned down—but he didn't. I used to take a lot of his bass lines for reference. We didn't have him out here originally, so if I wanted to do an arrangement and be really hip, I would keep a library of James Jamerson licks and I would use the ones that fit what I was doing. One time we were doing a thing with Shirley Bassey on a tune called 'I'm Not Anyone,' and he was taking pills because he was under medication. It was hard on him. Well, they turned the red light on and that man, he just rumbled. I started to break up a little bit emotionally. It was like thunder. There has been no bassist in R&B that has changed the concept of commercial music like James Jamerson."
>
> —GENE PAGE—
> West Coast arranger

"As far as I'm concerned, he was Motown."

—WAH WAH WATSON—
West Coast and former Motown session guitarist

"He was the first melodic electric bass player. Especially the Four Tops stuff. I don't know whether it was the group that brought it out in him—but like on "Bernadette"—the bass on that thing is serious. That is a hard bass line. There's still guys today who can't play that one. That gave me some trouble actually, because I used to play those parts on gigs."

STANLEY CLARKE
Bassist

"People were always telling James that he was way ahead of his time."

ANNIE JAMERSON

"Jamerson was the bass sound in the world . . . on the planet!! Cats all over the world were cutting and using his lines to make hits. In America they didn't know him that well, but in Europe they knew everything about him."

—MELVIN FRANKLIN—
Bass singer for the Temptations

Kudos

> "Jamerson changed the electric bass because he was a bass player. A lot of guys graduated from guitar to bass when electric bass came along. By him originally being a bass player, it felt like a bass. For drummers, there was something very special about playing with Jamerson."
>
> —JAMES GADSON—
> West Coast session drummer

> "A lot of people said that James had a lot to do with the Motown sound. James Jamerson had a lot to do with the sound of music—period. I know musicians all over the country who were trying to copy this guy. He was from another place; he was a creator; an innovator. When he played, it was a song within a song. When I first came to Detroit and started producing at Motown, Smokey, Holland—Dozier—Holland, and all the other producers all said, 'You got to get Jamerson on your sessions. He's the guy that makes it happen.'"
>
> —FRANK WILSON—
> Motown songwriter and producer

> "When Leo Fender designed the Fender Bass, he had James Jamerson in mind."
>
> —RON BROWN—
> West Coast session bassist for Motown

"*Engineers loved him because you never heard scratching or unwanted overtones from his bass.*"

—EARL VAN DYKE—
Motown keyboardist and session leader

"*Nobody ever knows genius when you're going by it. We found out later that he was a genius. The producers knew that he was necessary, but the business situation at Motown always superceded the talent.*"

—THOMAS "BEANS" BOWLES—
Motown saxophonist and manager and co-creator of the early Motor Town Revues

"*Jamerson had a reputation for being the hot bassist in town when he was really young. Everybody wanted to hear his bass. The first time I heard him play was in high school and it was one of the most gratifying times that I can recall. I had heard so much about him. When he came to Motown, I noticed that he could cause things to happen spontaneously by the lines that he played . . . he was a leader when it came to that.*"

—BRIAN HOLLAND—
Motown songwriter and producer

> "When Jamerson played through changes, it was incredible because he was so melodious with what he was doing. James didn't just play root and fifth. He played through the changes while keeping a great pocket."
>
> —DENNIS COFFEY—
> Solo artist and Motown session guitarist

> "What James contributed to the music was a sense of jazz as opposed to basic R&B. When he came on the scene in the early '60s, bass parts hung on the roots and fifths and then called it a day. So when he started elaborating, even his simple lines were far more complex than what anybody had been doing up to that time. He brought a jazz concept to the R&B world probably trying to make it more interesting to himself playing-wise, because if he had to play those stupid two beat bass parts all day on take #641, he'd go crazy. He also knocked me out because he was one of the first cats I ever heard do any octave types of things, which later became the bottom end of disco. The word 'genius' was thrown around a lot in reference to him by producers and songwriters at Motown."
>
> —DAVE VAN DEPITTE—
> Motown arranger

> "He set a standard for all pop bass players up until a decade ago when the new generation came in with the popping and slapping."
>
> —PAUL RISER—
> Motown arranger

> "He was solid all the way around. He made my job really easy. What he stressed to me was holding the pocket and the timing. 'Whatever you do' he said, 'make sure that when you come out of your fills, that you're right back in the groove. It's not how much you do. It's what you do.' You could depend on James' bass part every night."
>
> —LARRY TOLBERT—
> Drummer with Aretha Franklin and Ray Parker's Raydio

> "You could write it out for him and he would play it and improve upon it at the same time. It was like sight reading and improving upon it at the same time because he could see so far ahead in the piece."
>
> —ROBERT WHITE—
> Motown guitarist

> "I used to open some of the old Motown shows, and I also worked a lot with James at some of his club gigs like the Chit Chat and the Twenty Grand. He was the most hilarious and craziest person I ever met. You could see that when he was in that environment, it was his world. No matter what Jamerson was going through, he would get so involved in what he was playing that nothing else mattered. From watching him, he made me understand and believe in the power of music. It's the best therapy you can ever have."
>
> —ORTHEIA BARNES—
> Detroit television and radio personality

> "He was the only guy I ever saw who was just as adept on electric as he was on upright. He's really the father of the modern day bass player. He had the purest fingering—all his notes were true and pure. No matter how fast he was playing them or whatever rhythmic pattern he was doing, you could hear the whole note. That was a big part of his sound. Even today, nobody plays like that."
>
> —SMOKEY ROBINSON—
> *Motown composer and recording artist*

> "Jamerson was a genius."
>
> —MARVIN GAYE—
> *Motown recording artist*

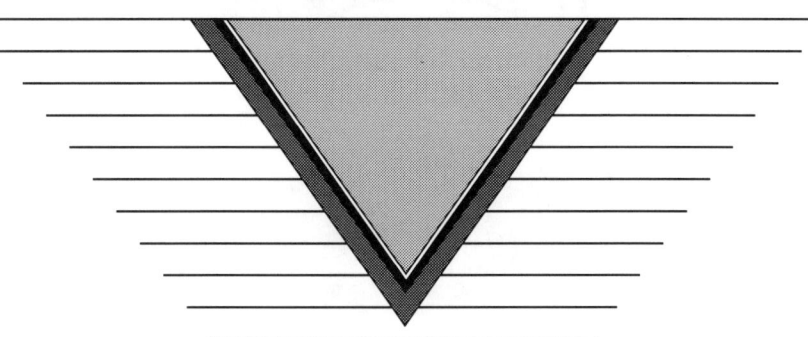

BIBLIOGRAPHY

FOOTNOTES

1) Nelson George, "Standing in the Shadows of Motown," *MUSICIAN* magazine, February 1987, Page 63.
2) Nelson George, "Standing in the Shadows of Motown," *MUSICIAN* magazine, February 1987, Page 62.
3) Nelson George, *Where Did Our Love Go?* (New York: St. Martin's Press, 1985), Page 110.
4) Nelson George, *Where Did Our Love Go?* (New York: St. Martin's Press, 1985), Page 110.
5) Nelson George, *Where Did Our Love Go?* (New York: St. Martin's Press, 1985), Page 109.
6) Don Waller, *The Motown Story* (New York: Charles Scribner's Sons, 1985), Page 158.

FURTHER LITERARY SOURCES

In addition to the books and articles cited in the footnotes, the following list comprises most of the printed material on James Jamerson's life and career:

1) Obituary, *CREEM*, November 1983.
2) Marshall Crenshaw, "James Jamerson: 1938—1983," *ROLLING STONE*, September 29, 1983.
3) "Final Bar," *DOWNBEAT*, November 1983.
4) Dan Forte, "James Jamerson—Preeminent Motown Bassist," *GUITAR PLAYER,* February 1983.
5) Nelson George, "Jamerson Will Be Remembered," *BILLBOARD*, August 1983.
6) "The Funk Brothers—Backbone of the Motown Sound," *GUITARIST,* January 1988.
7) "Editors Awards For Lifetime Achievement," *GUITAR PLAYER,* December 1985.
8) Hilary Clay Hicks, "James Jamerson Remembered," *MUSIC LINE*, December 1983.
9) Gerri Hirshey, *Nowhere to Run—The Story of Soul Music* (New York: Penguin Books, 1984).
10) Obituary, *JAZZ EDUCATION,* 1984.
11) Dave Marsh's *ROCK & ROLL CONFIDENTIAL*, August 1983.
12) Dave Marsh, "What Becomes of the Brokenhearted?" *RECORD*, November 1983.
13) Tom Mulhern, "20 Essential Bass Albums," *GUITAR PLAYER*, January 1987.
14) Don Snowden, "Motown's Unsung Hero," *THE LOS ANGELES TIMES*, August 28, 1983.
15) Obituary, *TROUSER PRESS*, November 1983.
16) Otis Williams, *Temptations* (New York: G.P. Putnam's Sons, 1988).
17) Mary Wilson, *Dreamgirl—My Life as a Supreme* (New York: St. Martin's Press, 1986).

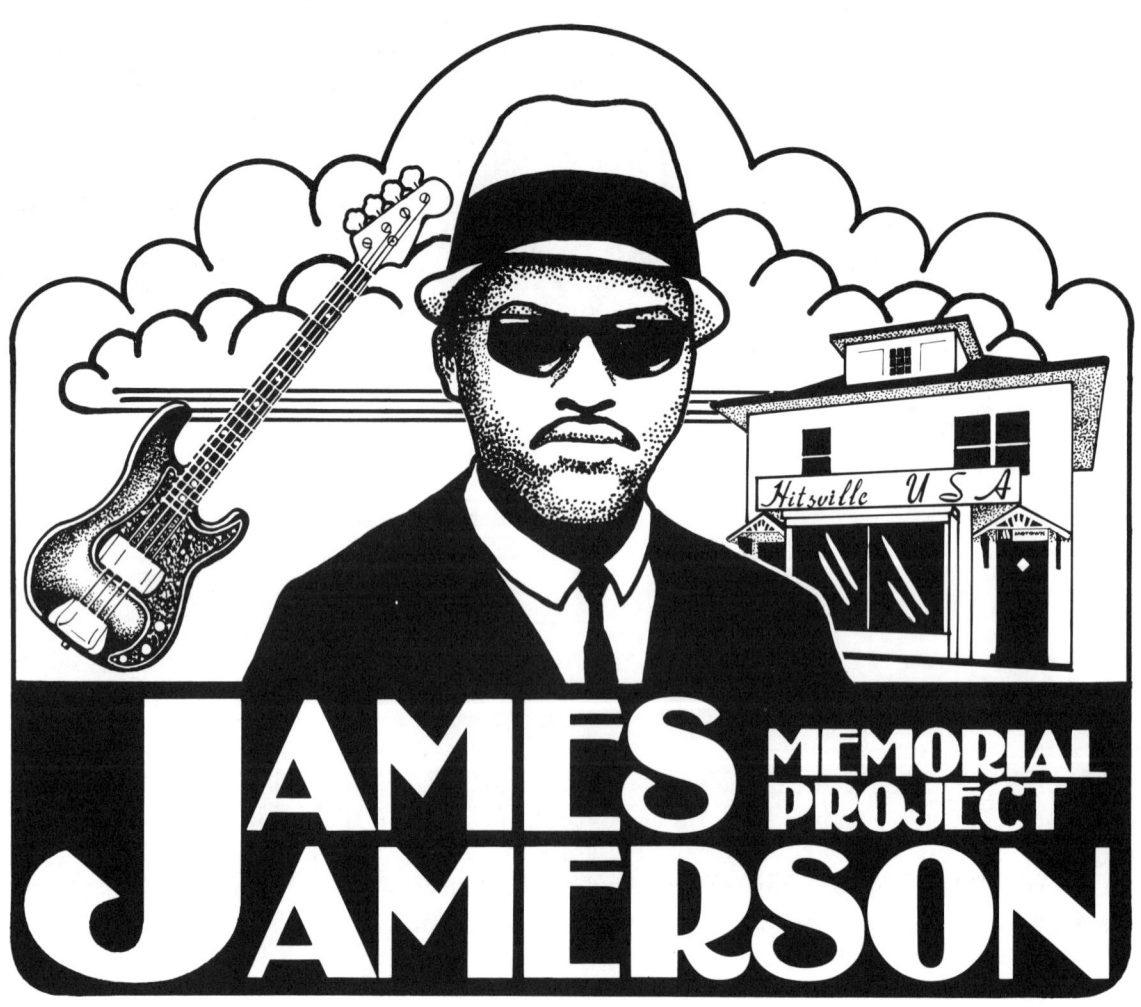

James Jamerson always felt indebted to Detroit's Northwestern High School because that was where his musical career had its beginnings. With your help, James is going home to his old alma mater to help build up its music program. In addition to directing some of the proceeds of this book to Northwestern, the Jamerson family and Dr. Licks Publishing are also hoping to raise additional funds for this project through the sale of James Jamerson photos, posters, T-shirts, and sweatshirts. We would also like to offer CD versions of the *Standing in the Shadows of Motown* tapes if there is enough demand.

If you're interested in any of these items, drop us a line and we'll put you on our mailing list. (Indicate which articles you're interested in.) We will get in touch with you when everything is ready. Send your inquiries to:

The James Jamerson Memorial Project
c/o Dr. Licks Publishing
327 Haverford Rd.
Wynnewood, Pa. 19096

Labella... The Only Strings James Jamerson Ever Used

E&O Mari LaBella
256 Broadway, Newburgh, New York 12550

Thanks James— For Realizing The Unlimited Potential Of The Fender Bass.

Fender®

"Sometimes I'd just look at a flower and the way it would sway would make me feel like playing a certain way..."

**JAMES LEE JAMERSON JR.
(JANUARY 29, 1936—AUGUST 2, 1983)**